Miner

A Life Underground

Thurman I. Miller

With

David T. Miller

Bacchante Books
Lexington, Kentucky

ISBN-13: 978-1514661314
ISBN-10: 1514661314

Dedication

This book is dedicated to the miners with whom I worked—those who taught me about coal mining and how to stay alive so far beneath the earth, and those for whom the mine became their final resting place.

Also by Thurman and David Miller:

War and Work

Coal Bloom

Suicide Creek

Always Faithful, Always Free

Earned in Blood: My Journey from Old-Breed Marine to the Most Dangerous Job in America

TABLE OF CONTENTS

Acknowledgements

In writing this book I have drawn on the memories of friends and former miners and deeply appreciate their support and interest in this project. As with all my prior books, my son David was and remains my coauthor and invaluable editorial assistant, doing everything from research and editing to writing the material that links my own life to its times, as well as handling photos, press releases, contracts, my website and much more; none of my books would exist without the countless hours he has put in on them.

My wife Recie, although she left this earthly plane several years ago, nursed me through my darkest years and I would never have survived the period I write about here without her; our bond still informs every page I write.

Thanks also to my son Gilbert Miller, a mechanical engineer, the Beckley Exhibition Coal Mine, Joy Manufacturing, Coyne Electrical School, The United Mine Workers of America, The Saturday Evening Post, authors Steve Flairty and Lynn Knapp Walters, the West Virginia and Regional History Center, the Mullens Area Chamber of Commerce, Arch Coal Company, the website www.coaleducation.org, West Virginia State Archives, Sally Watts, Joseph G. Anthony, the staff of the National Coal Heritage Area and especially Christie Bailey and Rachel McBride, soil scientist Dr. Willem van Eck, photographic specialist Tom Herrick, and miner and tipple man John Lewis.

Foreword

Returning home after his exemplary but draining service to his country as a US Marine during World War II Thurman Miller might justifiably have eased up a bit in the way he tackled life. He survived bombs, bullets, disease, dying buddies, and the constant, demoralizing stress of being smack dab in the middle of the most pivotal battles of America's war effort. Even after his service ended and he returned to his native West Virginia, he suffered the lingering effects of jungle-contacted malaria.

Enough is enough, Thurman might have rationalized. Let someone take care of *me* for a change. But that's not the way of the benevolent warrior, and he decided that with little thought. There were aging parents to care for and a young family to be raised and nourished. He needed a job to make it happen; mining coal wouldn't be a first choice, but, alas, it was essentially the only choice. Growing up around this way of life, he knew of the long, dogged man-hours, the poison and discomfort of coal dust, the knowledge that too many people who work underground will never come alive to the surface again.

For Thurman, it was all about duty and integrity. He had another job to do. This time it was as a miner, but it was still war.

In *Miner: A Life Underground,* Thurman Miller walks us, or should I say, *crawls us,* through the daily grind of almost forty years of relentlessly chasing after the hard black life source of coal. It's the mineral created by centuries in nature's underground pressure cooker. It keeps the lights on, but can drain a person's body and psyche until they're running on fumes. Thurman seeks no pity, yet helps us feel the unforgiving aches from both stooped and on-the-back labor; getting a few days off is only a temporary balm. Machinery breaks down, and more often than not, Thurman is the man who figures out how to do the fix—then does it, as a mechanic/electrician. He has a strong mind, a strong back, and his hands understand how to tame the magic of electricity.

The human toll of his occupation didn't stop when his military service ended. Tragic deaths in mine-related accidents are all too common in Thurman's second war. And this time he sees the pain in the eyes of his colleagues' families, their close friends, and, of course, deals with his own sense of loss as he bravely trudges forward, often by inches.

Now in his middle 90's, time seems to have dimmed neither his memory nor his spirit. Thurman's story presents a challenge to each of us: Given the hand that we each are dealt, how might we find such dedication, loyalty, creativity and sense of purpose in our own lives? The book you now hold captures the riveting account of how one soul, battered but unbowed, found a way forward from darkness into light. Now, let that message take wings in us, the readers.

Steve Flairty
Lexington, Kentucky

Steve Flairty is a writer, newspaper and magazine columnist, and retired teacher. He is the author of the book series *Kentucky's Everyday Heroes: Ordinary People Doing Extraordinary Things* and *Kentucky's Everyday Heroes for Kids* as well as the biography *Tim Farmer: A Kentucky Woodsman Restored.*

Introduction

During my years in the U.S. Marine Corps in 1945—my experience there is detailed in my previous books, especially *Earned in Blood*—whenever I was stateside and had a few days' leave I would make my way home to Otsego, West Virginia any way I could, including via train, bus and plenty of hitchhiking. After several years away, years spent fighting in the South Pacific, upon my discharge I had the luxury of my wife's father picking us up at the base. At once I felt a great load lifted from me, and at the same time all that I had seen and done came rushing back to me.

I was home only briefly before I simply passed out and remained unconscious for the better part of an hour. As I came to I saw my mother and Dr. B. W. Steele looking down at me. I heard him explain, "His nerves have been so elevated that when they started to taper off he did it suddenly; many returning veterans keep to a gradual descent."

I thus started my post-war adulthood from the lowest depths, mentally and physically. I spent many years thereafter avoiding an even further descent, and I began to seek some higher place, some livelihood in which I could raise a family.

Ironically, I found that higher place deep within the earth.

I never intended to become a miner. I had hoped to attend college after my military service, but money and jobs were scarce and I was chronically sick with malaria. I also had elderly parents to care for, and soon after I returned home my first son was born. Despite looking far and wide, I reluctantly came to the conclusion that coal was the only real way I could make money in my home state. And so I became a miner.

Mining is hard, dirty, strenuous work, even more so back then, before much of the back-breaking labor had been mechanized. But after I had worked in the mines a few months I began to gradually noticed, more and more, moments and then days of a new calmness. I gained confidence as an electrician and mechanic only slowly, but I found my mind gradually ceased to constantly replay the battles in which I had fought. The work I did required much concentration and I came to realize that being constantly busy and always learning are each a form of therapy.

Not every veteran of a brutal war is given the gift of realizing that the sorrow of thought is fed rather than drowned by intoxicants.

I have already written at length about my journey back from what we would now call post-traumatic stress with the patient help of my wife Recie; in this book I wanted to write about what miners actually *do*—or at least *did* during my tenure underground, roughly from the mid-1940's through the 1970's, which is all I can speak personally about. Mining has always changed more urgently than many other occupations because of the profit motive; technical improvements each year enable fewer men (and, now, women) to extract more coal more quickly. I can speak only of the days I spent underground, but I think the lessons I learned remain relevant.

How does a person learn to stay safe when literally the mountain above you conspires to compress your weak and contingent human form into the same strata of fossilized dinosaurs and million-year-old carbon we were digging up to sell? How does a human tame the bare ends of a copper wire that contains enough electricity to power a small town?

And, having gone underneath the mountain every day for years, why do some men prefer it to the safer, cleaner environs of above-ground jobs?

Perhaps it's the fact that as a cut of coal drops a miner can see minerals and the outlines of ancient organisms no human has ever seen before. Perhaps miners become addicted to the danger. For me, the challenge of those mining days were the balm I needed to heal my troubled mind and begin to clear the constant memory of my days making war.

I wonder still about what kind of redemption a man might find at the bottom of a mine shaft. I can't say that I know the answers to these questions, but I hope this book will give some insight to what a miner really does so that the reader can draw his or her own conclusions.

Illustrations

Please see the author's website for higher-quality versions.

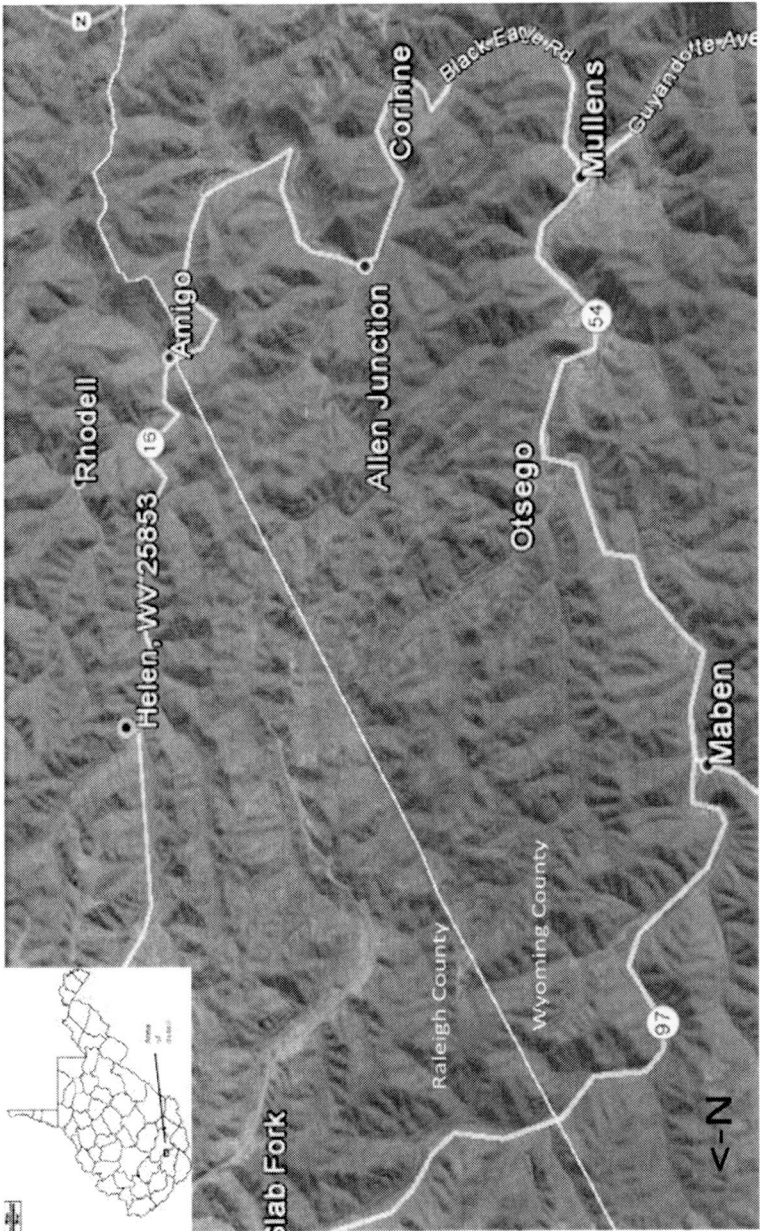

This is the area covered by this book, straddling Raleigh and Wyoming counties. Note that it is oriented eastward to match the underground mine maps.

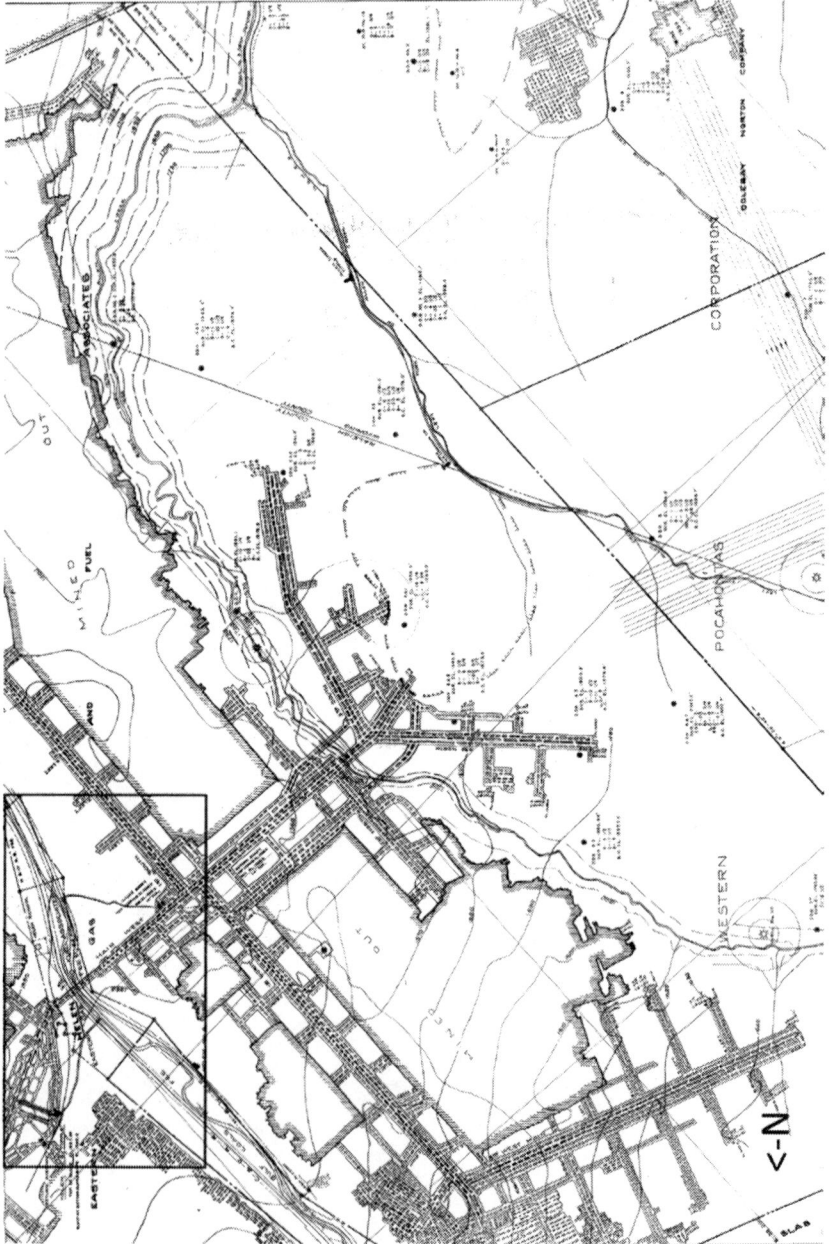

Underground mining map covering roughly the same area, also oriented eastward. The boxed area shows Helen, where I lived for fifty years. My hometown of Otsego is just off the page at lower right.

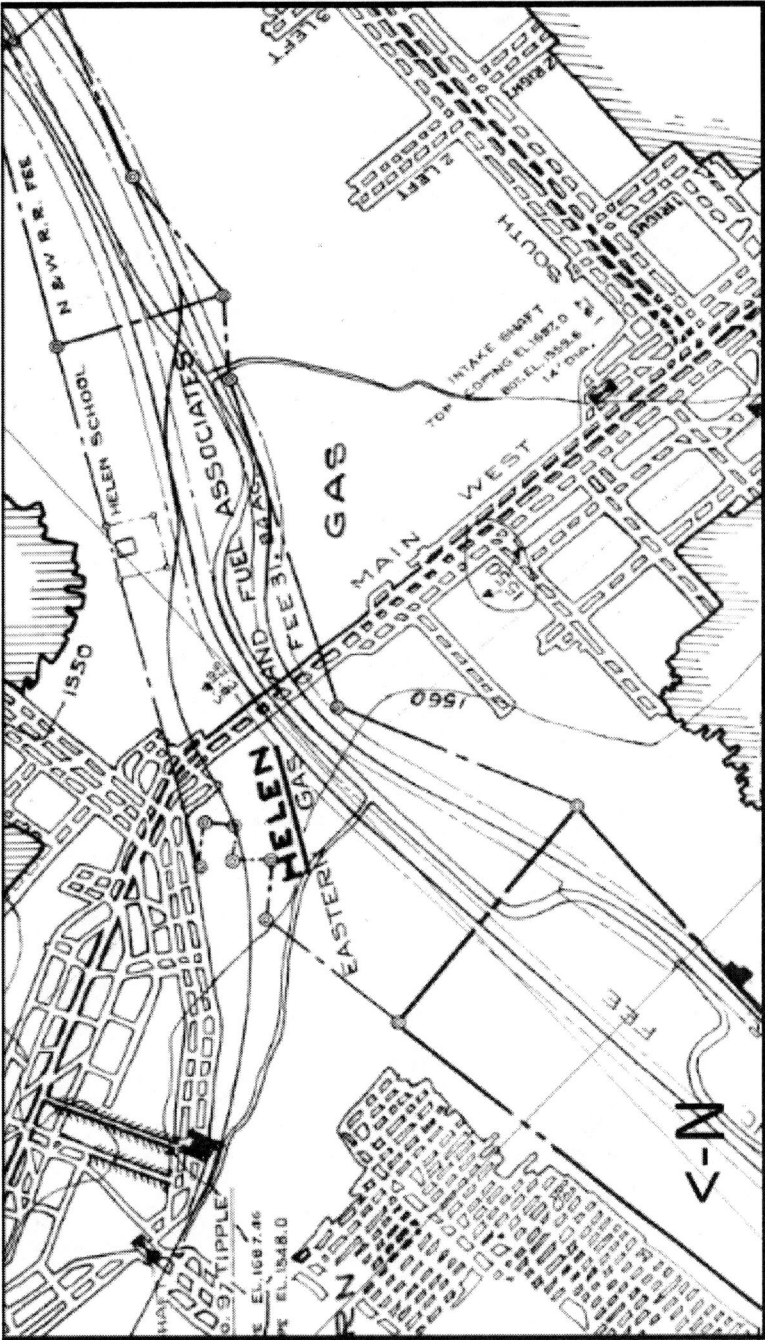

*Detail of the mines under the town of Helen,
from the preceding map.*

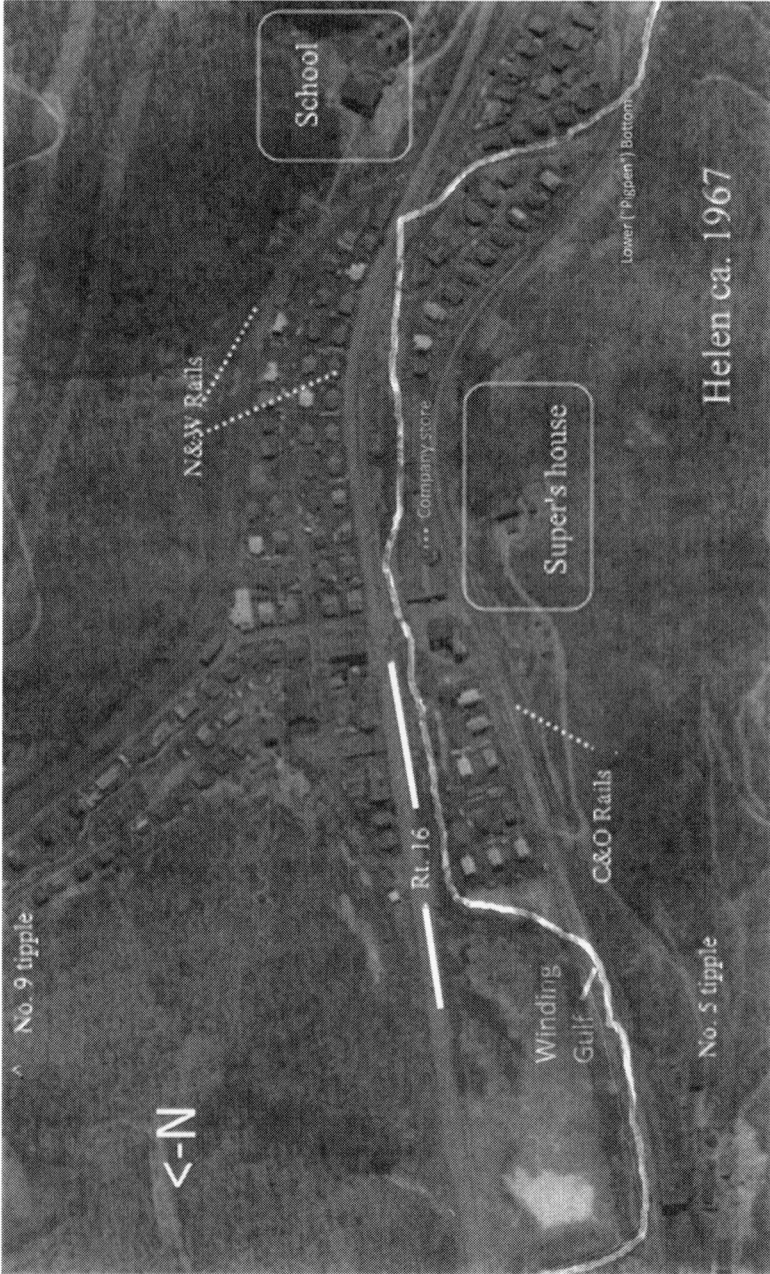

Above-ground view of Helen in about the same scale as the preceding map. As with virtually all coal towns the Superintendent house was located where he could observe the whole town.

Miner: A Life Underground

Chapter 1 – The Bounty of the Earth

Born in 1919, I grew up along Cedar Creek, outside Otsego, near Mullens, beside a seam of coal exposed by any flooding rain. Cedar Creek is part of in the Upper Guyandotte River watershed, which feeds into the Ohio and thence into the Mississippi.

The exposed seam showed thirty feet or so of high quality

I come from a large, blended family with many brothers and half-brothers, some a decade or more older than I. Since I was born in 1919 and many of them worked in and around the coal mine, it's not difficult to imagine them shoveling coal by hand in the early days of mining.

bituminous coal, there for the taking. Our very large and very poor family couldn't afford to ignore the free energy provided by the same earth we tilled on our subsistence farm.

My brothers would drill and shoot the seam with dynamite to loosen the coal and then shovel it onto the creek bank for the coming winter. Their method of digging the coal out was one many country folks used; they would lie on their side and dig into the bottom of the coal seam, making a cut about eighteen inches across, and then use a flat shovel, a "bug dust shovel," to dig down into the coal and shovel it into buckets. Our early home was just above the Otsego grade school and the opened coal seam was about 25 feet up the hill behind the house. My brothers built a small cart mounted on small truck wheels belonging to my brother Dewey. The narrow gauge track was made of wooden two-by-twos and was about fourteen inches wide.

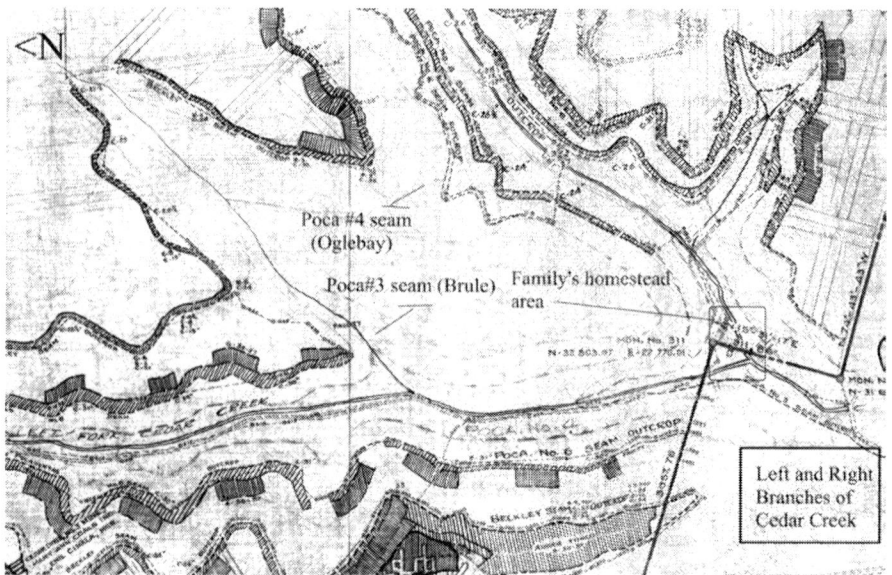

I grew up along Cedar Creek, just above Otsego. I would eventually work in mines on both sides of Cedar Creek, first for Brule and then for Oglebay Norton.

Fountain Sumner, my brother-in-law, lived further up the holler and also had an opening to .the same coal seam just above his house on Cedar Creek and mined it as my brothers did.

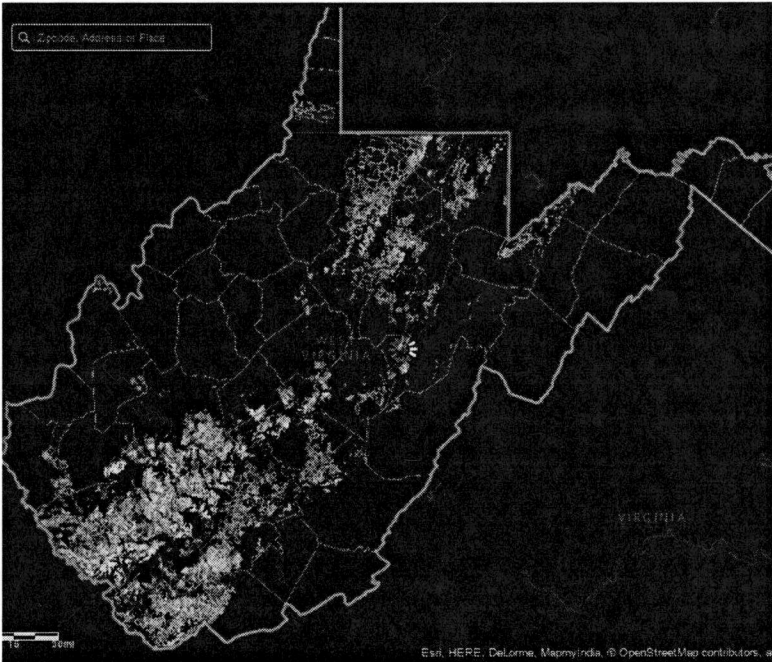

Highlighted areas show where coal is mined in West Virginia.

Small seams erupt everywhere in our narrow valleys here in the steep foothills of the Appalachias. Technically, in southern West Virginia we have no mountains, only valleys left behind by millions of years of erosion of an ancient sea bed; the eastern part of the state had much more of the geologic upheavals that produced true mountains. Because of these ancient geologic accidents coal isn't found throughout West Virginia, but only in the southwestern and to a much lesser degree the north-central part of the state.

Whether true mountains or not, they were mountains to me, and all around me. When I wasn't helping my Dad I'd just take off in the woods and spend the day roaming. Just as we couldn't ignore the free coal all around us, in the fall of the year I'd eat grapes, hazelnuts, anything growing wild, and I knew what all of it was, each plant. With a large family and many older brothers I had to supplement my meals with whatever else I could find growing nearby.

When I was a teenager I got a job hunting our cows in the evening. Several people then began to hire me to help with their cows. When harvest time came my cousin and her husband, who lived right up above us in the holler, hired me to cut corn, dig potatoes, and whatever else he needed done. At first he paid me a dollar a day but eventually he raised my pay to a dollar and a half per day. Big money for the time. I grew up poor, but it didn't bother me because it was all I knew, and the mountain and clear-running streams provided the basics of life for free.

Before there were bathhouses, and when indoor plumbing was still a relative luxury, miners resorted to the standard #3 washtub.

When I was fourteen (in 1933, the worst year of the Depression) we moved further up Cedar Creek about six hundred yards. A different section of the same coal seam still lay in the creek bottom beside our small house. Perhaps we stayed near it because not only could you dig enough to make the difference between a very hard and truly hard winter, you could get cash money for it.

I come from a very large, blended family. My only full brother, Buck, and my several half-brothers, most of whom who were a decade plus my senior, worked in the coal mines. I would listen as my older brothers spoke of their experiences in the mines—failing explosives, timbers breaking, how the mountain roared. They talked as many miners did, about how much coal they loaded that day or week. Sometimes it seemed from their bragging that they loaded more coal sitting there than they ever did in the mines.

Of course I could not understand at the time what they were discussing—tonnage, bad top, wet bottoms, drift mouths. But at an early age I formed a mental picture of life underground, especially as I saw the miners come home to bathe on their porch in a #3 washtub. I wondered if a job down in the mine would be my fate; I had little to compare it to, but gradually began to think perhaps I could escape the industry's pull.

One half-brother, Huey, worked the evening shift at the Otsego mine and rather than pack a lunch my mother would fix him a plate of food from our evening meal and dispatch me to deliver it to him. It was always dark on my return home and a half-mile trip along a deserted mountain road was a scary ordeal, out in the country in the pre-electricity 1920's. A twelve-year-old boy growing up in the country in that era was well aware that wildcats and other predators still roamed.

In the early 1920's the companies mining coal at Otsego still used mules, as was common then. Just a few hundred feet further up Cedar Creek there was a huge mule barn in which we children spent many a rainy day playing. One common story from that era is that after a large slate fall the superintendent asked, "How many mules did we lose?" By the time I began my career in the mines mules were no longer in use—humans were more easily replaceable.

Chapter 2 – Dirt Roads and Slate Dumps

I grew up roaming the mountain but consider the coal camp of Otsego, which lay in the valley just below us, my hometown. My own memories of living there reach back easily to the 1920's and 30's. Perhaps because of the shared danger of mining and the isolation of coal towns, families were closer to each other; there were no secrets to speak of. If a family hurt the community felt the pain. If a family fell on hard times the community knew about it and helped them.

But like every coal mining towns this one had its own personality. On any given day it could be benevolent and welcoming or it could rupture into anger at

A typical "street" scene in a typical coal mining camp. Between the dirt roads and the coal dust, everything acquired a layer of grime--including the residents.

some incident between families. This is perhaps inevitable in isolated towns where everyone knows everyone and there are no deep secrets. There were no drugs, little drinking, and surprisingly few fights among us youth.

It was a town of simple life, but it was a good life. A few families began to acquire radios. My cousin Walter Cook had one and during the warm summer evenings on Saturday he would throw open his front door and the window facing the porch and turn up the volume. A dozen or more of us young folks would gather outside, listening to the Grand Ol' Opry.

Without the distraction of a mass media we made our own amusement with birthday parties, lawn parties, and sandlot baseball. There were plenty of parties. We played games of our own invention, or spin the bottle, or any of hundreds of now-forgotten playground games. I attended a two-room school, which functioned as a community center, church, and more.

This 1937 National Archives photo of the Scotts Run coal camp could as easily be of Otsego, other than the paved road running through it. Note the ever-present haze of coal dust that got into everything, and everyone.

There was always tension between kids who lived in town and us "holler" kids. The layout of all coal towns from that era followed a strict pattern—one design fitted them all, taking into account landscape and the location of the mine's above-ground coal processing plant. Otsego was not large and was a typical coal mining town, consisting of about thirty-five dwellings. The town was laid off in a relatively wide bottom along Slab Creek.

On the right side of town in Otsego a row of three-room houses sat on the hillside and there was a narrow walking trail between the right row of houses and the ones on the hill. Two larger structures were set aside for the mine superintendent and mine foreman, with the Super's house situated to give him the broadest possible view of the entire town. Just a few hundred yards above the tipple between the road and Slab Creek was another row of houses which housed the black mining families.

In many coal towns there was barely any distinction between the mine and the town. This is near the Cassville mine, 1937. The privy on the left was built by the Works Progress Administration.

Our mother had Buck and me deliver milk to a black family that lived closer to the tipple and in winter the lady of the house always had us come in and warm ourselves.

Two rows of houses were built on the bottom and a row of houses on the hillside paralleling Route 54, which led south from Maben, Pierpoint, Lester, and Sophia, past Otsego and on to Mullens. I remember when Route 54 was just a gravel road. I was just a teenager when it was paved and my younger brother Buck and sisters Kathy and Gladys called it the hard road. We would walk down to it just to watch the shiny cars go by, as we dreamed of the larger world it led to.

Coming down Cedar Creek, crossing Route 54 into Otsego, one can still see the typical scheme of a coal mining town. The first house on the left typically defines the entire community, for all the houses were exactly alike. A wooden sidewalk would follow the length of the unpaved street. My Grandfather built his home directly across Slab Creek in Otsego. On the opposite side stood a two-story boarding house. I remember standing in Grandpa's backyard and watching that structure burn down.

The next row of coal camp houses would follow the same pattern, with a sidewalk and board fence on both sides. The Virginian Railroad track ran just beside, with the company store just across the track. Just after leaving high school I worked in the Otsego company store for a few months. Otsego's store was representative of so many others—we local miners were, in the time before decent roads, a captive audience; most transactions were still in "scrip" rather than cash, and the company deducted the usual, if inflated, charges for a doctor, union dues, insurance, store purchases, and so on.

The dollar, dime and quarter versions of one company's scrip, the private money we were paid in.

The focal point of any coal town was the company store. There is really no modern analogue for the company store.[1] It's hard to

---

[1] The centrality of the company store in Appalachia was a function of how remote the area was. According to the Encyclopedia of West Virginia, "In 1922, almost 80 percent of West Virginia miners lived in company houses and shopped in company stores, while only 10 percent of miners in Illinois did so....In West Virginia the company store served as a commercial center, a community center, and a formative influence on coal town culture...[T]he store building usually also included the post office and the payroll office. It served as a community center, and its architectural design, while functional, often revealed the cultural origins of its owner... Residents converged on the store shortly before the arrival of the mail to chat about work, train schedules, daily events, or family matters. After work, miners often congregated on the store porch after "drawing scrip," to review the day's work or talk of company affairs... The company store declined after mid-century with the spread of automobile ownership and the mass marketing of consumer goods through mail order catalogs and chain stores."

imagine, now, a town with little means of transportation other than the rails—owned by the same people who owned the town itself—and with its own private currency, like a small country of its own. Transportation was difficult and the company store offered credit against wages the miner had not yet earned—thus Tennessee Ernie Ford's song complaining that he "owed his soul to the company store."

"Breaker boys" like this one from the anthracite fields of Pennsylvania, were common in coal mining until well into the 20th century. They and the children who worked underground were known for their fierce independence and joined some of the first labor unions in the industry.

By the late 1950's, when I had moved to the coal camp of Helen, the coal company brought in the payroll in cash and distributed it on Saturdays, which meant the line of miners waiting at the back window the company store for their pay—nearly a thousand men strong at one point—snaked its way down the street and across the main highway.

With their mothers and fathers shopping at the company store I would also see boys who would go to work in the mines as soon as they were old enough. Where we lived there was no other industry. Mining has a long and sordid history of using, and using up, very young kids. According to a Mine Safety and Health Administration report:

"In the early years of the 20th century, children as young as eight years old worked in the coal mines. The work was hard and the 'little boys' grew old and stooped before their time. An 1885 law required boys to be at least twelve to work in the coal breakers and at least fourteen to work inside the mines. A 1902 law raised the age to fourteen to work in the breakers. Although child labor laws did not allow children under fourteen to work in the mines, some states did not have compulsory registration of birth.

An eight-year-old British miner from 1908.

Boys were passed off as 'small for their age…'"

Boys worked in mines as nippers and spraggers and outside as breakers. Spraggers " controlled the speed of the mine cars as they rolled down the slope, slowing them with pieces of wood. They worked in pairs. Each boy had twenty or thirty sprags and as the mine cars rolled downhill the spraggers ran alongside the cars and jabbed the sprags into the wheels."

More young coal miners from the nineteen-teens. These worked in northern mines but could easily be my older brothers.

The job was as dangerous as it sounds. The car could fly out of control and jump the track and crash into the mine wall if the wheels were not spragged properly.

The best job for a boy was mule driver. He would drive through the mine coupling full cars together and leaving empties behind. As MSHA put it, "a good mule driver...had no problem obtaining a job as a miner when he was older." Despite the coming of child labor laws and the dramatic expansion of mine safety rules after World War Two, my own memories of the 1920's and 30's are that it was nothing extraordinary for boys to be employed in and around the coal mines even before their teens.

Chapter 3 – I Meet My Match

I met my future wife Recie (pronounced Ree-see) when we were both very young. Recie's parents, Dewey Marshall and Laura Tobler Marshall migrated to my little town of Otsego in about 1927. Dewey had worked in a furniture factory and Laura had been employed by the R.J. Reynolds Tobacco Company in Winston-Salem, North Carolina. Recie was four years old when they moved and I knew her from a very young age because when her younger sisters, Mae and June, were babies I was dispatched to deliver milk to the family.

Laura had been purchasing milk from a farmer who lived close by but one day when he came with the milk she had no money to pay so he refused to leave the milk. Laura took her problem to my mother, whom she knew because our family was so large in Cedar Creek and Otsego.

Kids who lived in the town, such as it was, had regular, painted houses supplied by the coal company. Those of us who lived in the "holler" might live in a house like this, built with what we could find or make.

We were already selling milk to a few families. When Laura explained to my mother she had no money at the time to pay my mother told her that was all right, those babies needed milk and she could pay when she could. If she was in a position to help, my mother never turned down anyone who needed a hand. That's when I began delivering the milk to the Marshalls.

At this time, in the early 1930's, there were only three houses and the old company store in that section of Otsego. Recie would have been about eight and I was four years older and I only saw her occasionally, as I would just knock on the door and hand over the milk to whomever answered, usually Laura.

When Recie was about twelve she and her mother both contracted typhoid fever and were quarantined for quite a while so I had little contact with the family for a year or two or until they both were declared well clear of the fever. Recie grew into a teen and as we played at the old school house at the confluence of the two Cedar Creeks, which was a sort of gathering place for young people during the summer months, I began to notice her more and more.

Her auburn hair had grown down well below her shoulders and she had developed into a beautiful girl. The first date I had with her, Dewey thought I had come to visit him. On our next date it dawned on him what was going on and at about eight o'clock he wound their small grandfather clock and made her go to bed. Slightly miffed, I walked to Caloric to see another girl I had my eye on and declared the end of that evening at nine o'clock. So much for my youthful courtships.

Recie

As time went by I would see her every morning when we caught the school bus. She seemed to be a bit embarrassed to talk to me in the presence of the other kids so I didn't press it. Times being hard, and Dewey and Laura scraping by perhaps a little less well than the rest of us, the sole of one her shoes hung loose and I told her later I would fix it if she would come to our house. Said she would be too ashamed to do that. But none of us "holler kids" or even the town kids were very well dressed so I thought little of it. We dated all through our school years and I subtly put the word out to the rest of the boys in the town: "Hands off Recie, she's mine." During high school I had two jobs, putting up the flag and taking it down after school, and when the mail came I had to sort it and deliver it to each teacher's room. Any time I took a letter to Recie's class I made it a point to walk by her desk and smile.

On May 19, 1939, I graduated from Mullens High School. After graduation I worked in the company store for a while, then hired on with the power company and then with the New Jersey-based Interstate Equipment Company, building an aerial tram for waste disposal near Montgomery, but when we finished that job the foreman told me he had no more work in the state; I could relocate to Pennsylvania if I wanted more. I didn't feel I could pick up and move at the time. I worked briefly in the company store. Our company store's manager was named Pendry and one day he told me not to ring up any more sales—some money was missing and the tally was not quite right. I knew the woman who was making the mistakes but I said nothing. I told him to rest assured, I would not touch the register any more, and at end of day I quit. Next morning he walked up to our house and wanted to know why I quit. "I won't work for a man who accuses me of stealing."

That was the end of that.

[2]I saw the smoke of approaching war over my beloved hills. I knew we would soon be at war with Germany and Japan, the news reaching even into our hollers. I decided to enlist before I was drafted, and spent five years in the Marine Corps, an adventure I have written about extensively in my other books.

After I returned stateside for retraining and rest after the ordeal of Guadalcanal and New Britain Recie and I announced our

---

[2] After I came home from the Corps Arnold Ball was store manager and hired me again, but a few weeks later a boy from Pierpoint, who had been working there when he was drafted, came home and reclaimed his job--that was the law then, a soldier's job was his when, or if, he returned.

engagement and married July 30, 1944. The *Enola Gay* and its atomic cargo brought an end to the war and my fear that I would be among the soldiers invading Japan.

After I was discharged Recie and I came home to Otsego and began building a small house for us. We would part only on her death, sixty-four years after our marriage and three children later. She would nurse me through the darkest days of my life, as I gradually recovered from the degradations of war, as I gradually learned to be as a coal miner and father. Her patience in each of these was boundless and a gift of grace far beyond what any of us could ask for in this world.

Chapter 4 – Higher Education

I had been in boot camp at Parris Island only a short while before I began paying attention to the instructors as they snatched a rifle from a recruit. Their eyes never wavered away from the platoon as they went from one order to the next. Always when the platoon was ordered "fall in" it was automatic for our weapon to be thrust butt down at our right foot. When the order "left arms" sounded we stood at attention and the instructor began his rifle inspection. His eyes stayed locked on the recruit's eyes until he grabbed the rifle to inspect it; after he saw that it was well-maintained he threw it back to the recruit, the instructor's eyes on the recruit's as he caught his rifle.

Especially after being promoted to PFC, I began to study the men around whom I would serve for much of the five years. I learned that by simple observation I could infer a great deal about a man's personality, his attitude towards the Corps and his potential reliability in combat. Many had a better education than I, though I was their superior officer. I learned to adjust my questions and replies to their level, whatever it was.

One by one I sought some commonality with each man and when the opportunity arose I would have an extended conversation with him. As I came up in ranks to corporal and then sergeant and assumed responsibility I found this practice to be a great help in establishing mutual respect between myself and the men in my platoon—with of course an exception now and then in which I needed to pull my rank.

This was especially true in the South Pacific, where any small mistake I might make in reading a man could lead to the death of many more. I tried to tuck this lesson away, not knowing where I would need it, but knowing I would—and I did, in the mines.

Otsego was never far from my thoughts during my time in the Corps. The Otsego schoolhouse mentioned above was the gathering place for the community and there was no discrimination as to denomination. A "holy roller" could and did preach if he desired. Of course there was a regular minister, a Presbyterian since the principal of the school Effie "Granny" Delp was of that faith. His name was Currie. After I joined the Corps he sent me a small red Bible which I placed in my pack. After landing on Guadalcanal I was sitting on the beach during a short lull of activities and idly got the little testament out. Sitting there on the edge of hell I asked myself, what's purpose of it all?

When I opened the little red book it happened to reveal the gospel of John: "Greater love hath no man than this, that he lay down his life for his friend." As was true in the bright, lush, deadly South Pacific tropics, I would come to learn, was true in the darkest depths of the coal mine.

Chapter 5 – Into the Earth

After my September 24th, 1945 discharge from the Marine Corps I came home to Otsego and searched for work, to no avail. I went pretty well all over the region, to the telephone company in Charleston, to the Celanese plant in Narrows, Virginia, and many others.

I needed a job to go to each day; I had a purpose, to provide for Recie—and soon to provide for our son, Gilbert. But it was hard to see past the immediate darkness. For the moment, my main goal was to stay alive, as my body was still wracked with the pain and nausea of malaria as well as the psychic wounds of the war.

I finally decided if I were to remain in my mountains of WV it would be in the coal mine, for there is where the money was. I went to work on the same mountain where I had taken Huey's supper to him and was hired as a mechanic/electrician helper—although my formal certification for that position came only many years later.

Mining was not the college education I had wished for, but it was an education nonetheless. From my start in the mine I spent almost two years on the "hoot owl" shift, working midnight to the early morning and sleeping, or trying to.

I stood there ready to enter the mine on the conveyor belt that first day and my mind harkened back to an earlier visit to this same mine while I was still a marine. I remember looking down at my spit-shined shoes, the perfect crease in my spotless uniform. I watched the grimy men as they came out of the mine, their eyes permanently ringed with black. I asked myself *how and why in the hell do they do this?* I was to find out.

Riding into the mine for the first time felt like it did as I approached the island of Guadalcanal on a troop transport ship. It was not fear which stabbed my heart but anxiety, the unknown.

That first day, and every day thereafter, I hung my brass check with my designated number on the check board at the mine entrance. This system showed who was in the mine, in case of a disaster; brass has a high melting point.

When the conveyor belt reversed and the men began to climb on it I watched how they did it and climbed on behind Huey. The black hole came toward me and I felt like I was heading for a beach landing, not knowing what lay ahead.

Danger comes in the thinking. When the mountain roars its fury a miner may find a solid block of coal to run to. He thinks, *I will be buried here and no one will know.* On a sandy beach about three months into Guadalcanal I sat still, observing my fingernails. And they moved. Thinking it strange I began to just pluck them off one by one. Removing my boots, the same thing with my toenails. Then it sank in: *I am slowly dying.* These thoughts returned, unbidden and unwelcome.

I went to work at a mine at Otsego in October 1945, first as a mechanic helper. Coal seams occur at varying depths and I started on the Beckley seam, which was the geographically highest seam, i.e., closer to the surface. After a few months I was transferred to the Number 3 seam, opposite the tipple. (See the map in the set of illustrations above for where these mines lay in relation to Otsego and to Cedar Creek.) I stayed at that seam until the late fifties, when I transferred to the Number 4 seam, on the opposite hillside. All told, I would work in an Otsego mine for nineteen years.

I was not thinking of the future, however; for now I had to learn the very basics of being a miner. I watched my brother Huey's every move that first month. Taking his hammer and sounding the top, being careful to set a timber under a dangerous hanging roof, making sure the power was off when starting an electrical check, safely riding and exiting the belt, keeping tools squared away and clothes tucked in while riding the belt, and so on. I quickly realized that, as in war, you don't get a first chance to make a mistake and learn from it; your first mistake may be fatal.

From Huey and many other experienced miners I learned, and applied what I learned. As in the Corps, I always studied the faces of the foreman to see what their expression told me. Sometimes it was hostility and sometimes they would patiently explain what the problem was. I came to realize how much alike the two very different segments of my life were, and that what I learned as a Marine I applied unthinkingly to my tenure as a coal miner.

I also learned the importance of directing a constant fresh air flow to the remote areas of the mines in which you were working. There are three main entries into a mine, with the beltline in the middle of the three. The other two are for the intake air and return or exhaust air. An exhaust fan outside the return air opening draws fresh air from the surface, delivers it to the working area via a series of curtains, and back out the exhaust.

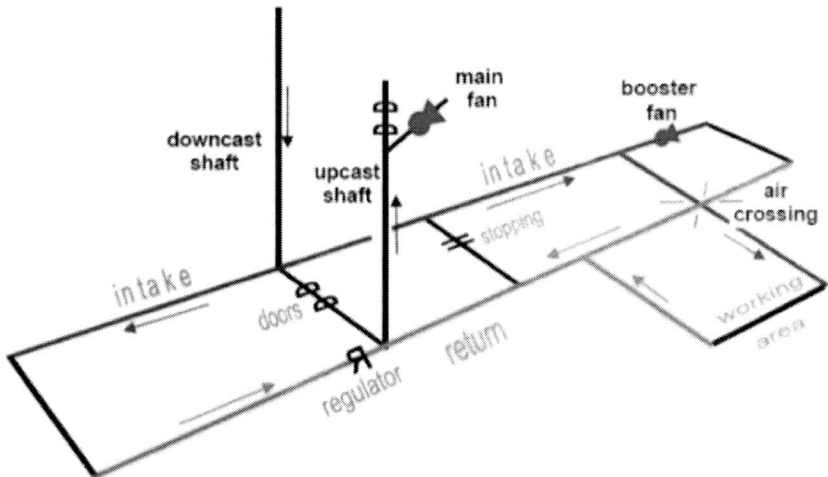

Fresh air is delivered into the deepest working part of the mine, the face, through large exhaust fans and a complex system of fabric curtains or more permanent barriers. Constantly moving air is the best defense against a buildup of methane.

I had much to learn about mining. Mines have to be planned and executed methodically in order to create a straight entry, with "breakthroughs" turned left and right at the proper intervals to maximize the amount of coal that can be extracted. Back then, before high-tech engineering methods, it was both an art and a science. (In the early "coal rush" days old-timers like Spink Farley could walk a mountain and suss out where the best coal lay by the darkening of the soil where a seam of coal would "bloom.")

In the days when mules did the heavy pulling and undercutting of the coal, so it could be shoveled out, mining was a slow process but by the time I went into the mines much of the process had been

standardized. Coal companies employed engineers whose main job was to plan straight, precise routes for the "rooms" that became the miners' work areas. They used the same type of transits as land surveyors and placed "spads," pieces of flat metal sharpened on one end and with a hole in the other, into the top of the roof of the chamber. They used a small handheld drill to make a hole about three-quarter inches into the roof and cut short pieces of dowel the same diameter, and drove the spad into the wood; leaving the hole to hang a plumb-bob on. (I still have one of these spads from early in my career when an engineer got me to be his helper.)

A spad.

Meanwhile, the engineer would set up his transit under a previously-set spad and plumb-bob. His transit was set so he could just see the very bottom of it. The helper would hold his plumb bob up against the top and the engineer would indicate where to drill the hole, and the helper would hang a plumb bob on the next spad about six feet further into the mine entryway. The engineer would line them and motion the helper to use his hammer and tap the spad either left or right until the tips were exactly in line.

When a foreman needed to "check the centers" he would have a face man put a small piece of paper over his head lamp. The foreman would then get behind the two spads and line them up with the miner's lamp and motion for him to mark the top with chalk. If the chalk mark was very close to the center of the entry the foreman knew he was going straight.

A plumb-bob.

When working with high-voltage electricity in wet, dark conditions, even the most everyday situations can result in a fatal accident or bad injury. As in the military, the mines relied on a type of buddy system. Two or three men would remain in contact as they worked, watching for danger from all quarters. An experienced miner could spot a dangerous situation before it developed into a deadly one. A loose piece of rock, an unsecured swing loader boom, an oncoming buggy.

After becoming a shift leader I found myself sometimes speaking with my Gunny voice, which I had trouble controlling. As on the domestic front, I had to make myself remember: *You're not a Marine now, you're just a miner.* But some military practices seemed ideal for my civilian job. In the Corps we were taught to field strip our weapons, doing this over and over until we became

Setting timbers, and learning how to read the mountain as they gradually snapped, was a matter of life and death.

so familiar with our pieces we could do it blindfolded. The instructors taught us to lay out each piece from left to right so when we had to do this in total darkness the last piece we took out was the first re-installed, left to right. I kept to the same method when breaking down and rebuilding a complicated piece of machinery.

Early on in my career, before mines had separate transport systems for men, we rode the same reversible belt into and out of the mine that carried coal to the surface. Riding a belt line many feet down to the working area sometimes took the better part of a half hour, and if the belt was empty of coal, some men who had not had enough sleep would be lulled into slumber by the steady hum and rocking of the belt. It's hard to believe a man could be so relaxed, but easy to believe he would be that tired.

This detail from an underground mine map shows the importance of setting a straight line as the mine is being opened; some passageways go for thousands of feet. The small rectangles are pillars of coal left behind to support the roof until the rest of the coal is mined out, then the coal in the pillars is mined and the roof permitted to fall in.

Once, we were on our way down and were riding the first mainline belt, which was about 2600 feet long, the typical length of an entryway, probably based on the capabilities of the available technology at the time. At the tail-piece of this belt another main line belt was installed so coal would just dump off from it onto the next belt. The tail-piece of belt one extended some six feet back under the head roller of number two, with only about six inches of space between them.

About fifty feet before reaching the jump-off point I got to my knees and dismounted. I walked a few feet, turned and saw a man still riding just a few feet from the head roller of belt two.

Realizing he was asleep I quickly grabbed his collar and unloaded him as if he were a piece of timber. He scrambled to his feet, sleepily ready for action. Upon seeing how close he came to death he just shook his head and looked at me and grinned.

The belt line in the mine I started in was about 24 inches wide and had a middle roller in the center and one on either side, sitting at about a forty-five degree angle, making the belt high enough on each side so that coal would be easily transported without much spillage. I watched the men get off the running belt at the tail end of the belt line that carried men and supplies to where we would work.

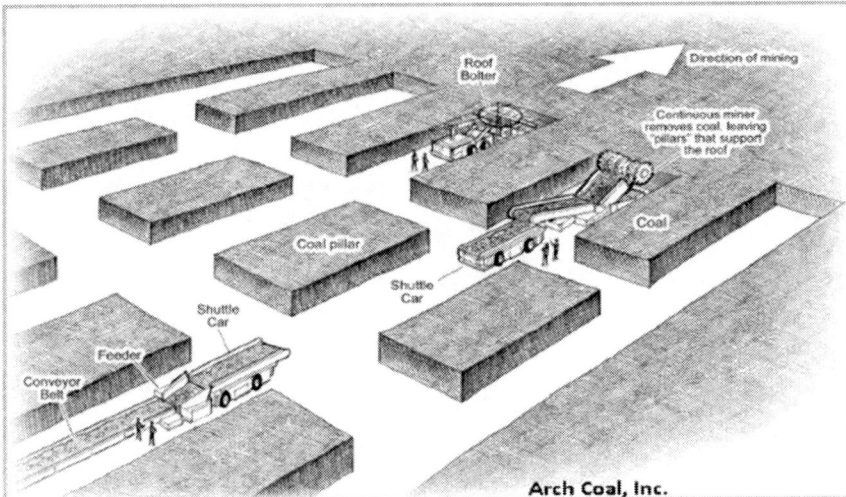

This diagram shows how an underground mine typically progresses.

I learned many safety basics from Huey, especially to pound the rock above me to check for a hollow sound, which indicated the need to set timbers. This was the most important early lesson I received about coal mining—to constantly know the difference between good and bad top. I first had to learn how the many tons of rock over a miner's head are supported.

I had been with Huey only a month when I was taken off the maintenance crew before I was transferred to the Number 3 seam as a belt cleaner. I did not like this job but kept it until sometime in 1947. I still had constant recurring nightmares and intrusive thoughts that took me back to the South Pacific but I was willing to learn. I admit I was terribly ignorant as to *how* to work. I knew nothing of machinery and its maintenance, and the work I started with was so boring I wished for something to make me think. In doing so, I thought, I could begin burying the past. But I also had nightmares about being buried myself, either completely or as casually as the dead Japanese soldiers I saw washed up on the sands of Guadalcanal.

The belt cleaning duty in the Number 3 mine put me in much lower coal, averaging about thirty two to forty-eight inches high, but in some cases as low as twenty-eight inches, too low for even the smaller cutting machines. This was a much harder job than the maintenance work and it soon began to take its toll on me, for I was still in the grip of recurring bouts of malaria and other tropical diseases I brought home as war souvenirs.

One malarial episode put me in the VA hospital in Huntington for twenty-one days. I applied for work in the mine again and this time I was hired on at the same mine as my brothers Lee and Buck. Our job was to shuttle supplies into the mine. One man loaded timbers, rock dust or whatever the list called for, and my job was to transfer all this, once it reached the base of the main belt line, to the belts that fed the cross-sections.

Each section belt head had a spill plate mounted on the side of the main belt and I

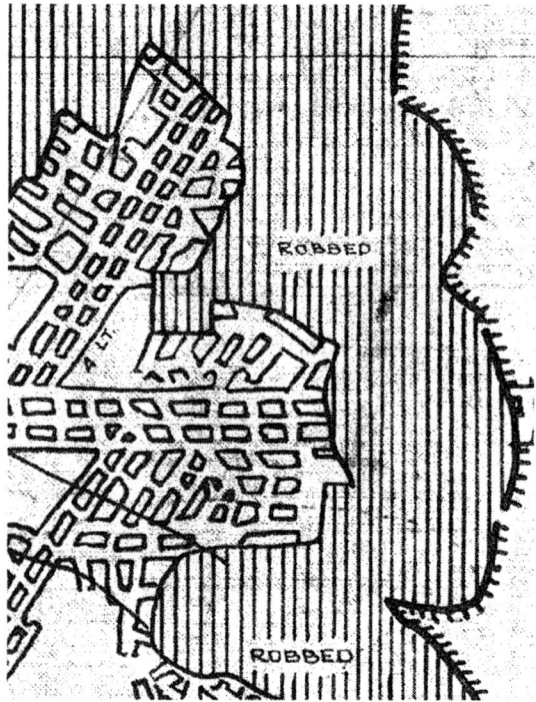

Once the coal has been mined from the mine section the coal remaining in the roof-supporting pillars is also mined as the workers retreat. This can lead to some tricky situations as the roof begins to collapse. This area has been "robbed" of available coal.

would grab the front end of a timber and put it upon the section belt head, which was running in reverse, while Lee was at the tail piece taking everything off.

Buck worked at a belt head toward the outside and as he followed the "all" board he and I went up to where Lee was working at the tail piece. We finished the shift by taking the pan line—the conveyor system which transports coal to the belt conveyor or a coal car and then out of the mine—apart and pushing the heavy pans to the mouth of the worked room. This was hard work; many times I would be in such pain I would crawl over out of the way and just lie down.

I was fortunate to be with Buck and Lee for they understood my condition. He knew how much I had left over from World War 2, from my time in the Marines in the South Pacific. I had visions of dead Japanese soldiers sliding by on the coal belt.

I would go home to Recie, who nursed me through all the bad times, and I would be able to eat only toast and a little coffee before collapsing into bed. I would startle awake in the middle of the night, sure that we were being fire on and I had to reach my rifle. Or, worse, I wouldn't wake until I heard her scream, as in my restless sleep I confused her loving grasp with the grapple of a Japanese soldier who'd invaded my foxhole. These scenes repeated over and over, fading only over several years as an old photograph might.

When a section is being driven up it usually reaches a length of about 2600 feet. There are usually three entries being driven as it goes forward, and on each side of the belt line "rooms" are mined to a length of about three hundred feet. This leaves many "pillars" of coal in place to provide roof support.

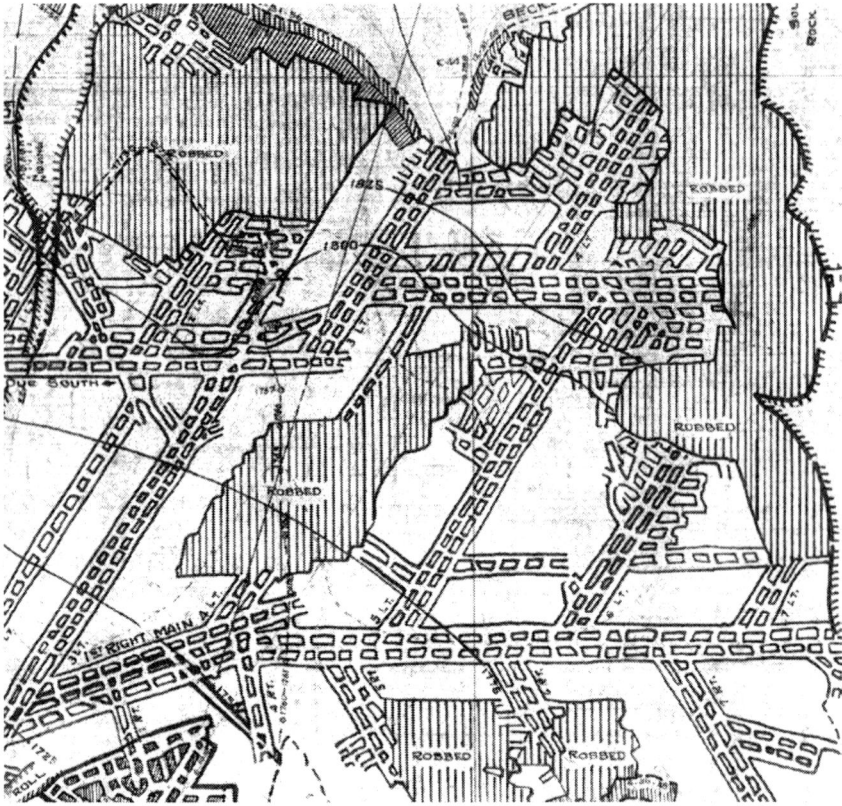

Detail from an underground mine map. A mine might have dozens of different sections, on several levels. Think you could find your way around?

In one of the mines I worked in, after the entry reached 2600 feet the machinery was put into action mining these pillars. This naturally leaves a large area mined out with only timbers holding up the mountain. As the weight begins to settle on the timbers they begin to bend and break.

I recall seeing one timber that was cut from green wood, and a few living but doomed green tendrils reached up toward the dim light bulb hanging just above. Funny substitute for the sun, I thought.

Miners learn quickly what the many tons of rock above them are composed of. Some are solid sandstone and it takes a lot of mining before this type will begin to break up and fall—as a matter of fact, sandstone will bend. I have witnessed a large worked-out area where one could look perhaps a couple of hundred feet and see the bend in the stone, as one can actually see the curvature of the earth far out at sea. When this type of cover finally has enough space and weight to cause it to fall it will break up as a plastered wall.

Some mines had what were termed as slate top. This type fell in very quickly but mostly as a controlled fall. Some seams have what miners commonly called "draw rock," and this kind of top presented a greater danger than others because it had a tendency to just break and fall between the timbers and mostly without warning. I witnessed all of these types of tops.

There were also "kettle bottoms," actually petrified tree stumps. They sat on top of the coal seam and appeared as just part of the roof but eventually, as the coal around them was removed, became very visible and dangerous, for when they fell they did so quickly and in one piece. They were among the most dangerous roofs.

Rites Set Today For Mine Victim

MADISON — Funeral services for David Ray Snodgrass, 42, of Racine will be at 2 p.m. today in the Leonard Johnson Funeral Home Chapel at Marmet. Burial will be in the Pineview Cemetery at Orgas.

Snodgrass was killed instantly Wednesday when a "kettle bottom" fell from the roof of the Omar Mining Co. Chesterfield Mine No. 1 near here, crushing him to death.

The bottoms of these petrified tree stumps were exposed as the coal fell away and the largest I saw was at least seven feet across the middle. (Needless to say I measured it only after plenty of timbers were set beneath it to prop it up.)

A mountain will begin to growl with the breaking of strata far up in the rock and many feet away. Miners long ago learned to "read" the mountain by the amount of thunder it creates, like counting the seconds between lightning bolts in a thunderstorm.

The top of a mining "room" is often supported by a series of "crib blocks," six by eight by twenty-four inches. These are built pig pen style across the entry, aligned with the solid block of coal.

When the mountain decides to break it begins with a low rumble as the rock above begins to settle, until finally the full weight comes crashing down and breaks in a straight line along the crib blocks. It is a sound one never forgets.

Slate falls are responsible for many injuries, minor to lethal. I vividly remember one man, a machine man or driller, standing by where a coal cut had just been completed and the coal and was ready to be hauled out. The cutting machine was being pulled back from the face. Suddenly a large piece of slate fell on him, about four feet wide, seven feet long and around five inches thick.

A cutting machine leaves about six inches of fine coal in the bottom and when the rock fell on him his body sank down into the fine cuttings. This helped keep much of the weight off him, but he was in much pain and still in danger. I happened to be close by and saw that the whole crew was confused as to what to do. I realized that the rock was too heavy for them to lift so I put two men gathering timbers and sent one to get a lifting jack.

They calmed down enough to begin doing what I told them and in a few minutes had the jack under the rock and began lifting it up while the crew started shoving timbers under the slate fall. We were able to extract the man from under it but he was hurt pretty badly, and was unable to continue to work. He died just a few years later.

After I had been working in the mines as a general laborer for about two years the chief electrician asked me if I would be interested in the maintenance force. I told him I would give it a try. He said for me to buy a few tools and I could add whatever else I needed as time went on. Next evening as I prepared to enter the mine I asked him who I was going with, "Hell," he said, "if there was someone for you to go with I would have sent him!" So I was on my own, knowing nothing about what I was getting myself into.

I was sent to a section with six conveyor units that were down, apparently because of a bad starting box on the Jeffrey cutting machine. This included six ten-horsepower pan line units, six five-horsepower units, and all the cables needed to run the equipment. I was responsible for all of it. The chief gave me a finger board, a control cylinder and a reverse bar to change out in one of the cutting machines.

I had never seen any of these before. My brother Buck, the belt man on that section, asked me what I was going to do. I told him I would fix it and he said, "Bet it won't run after you get done with it." I told him, "Don't bet the farm on it." I found the starting box, never having seen one before, and proceeded to remove the bolts holding the lid on. I looked it over and fortunately the old parts were still in the machine and I smiled. Piece of cake, I thought.

I unbolted the finger board, set the new one in my lap and proceeded to remove one wire at a time. I put the new one in the same place. All this took most of a shift. I finished and put the lid in place and plugged in the cable and started the machine. It worked! What an achievement for a greenhorn, I thought.

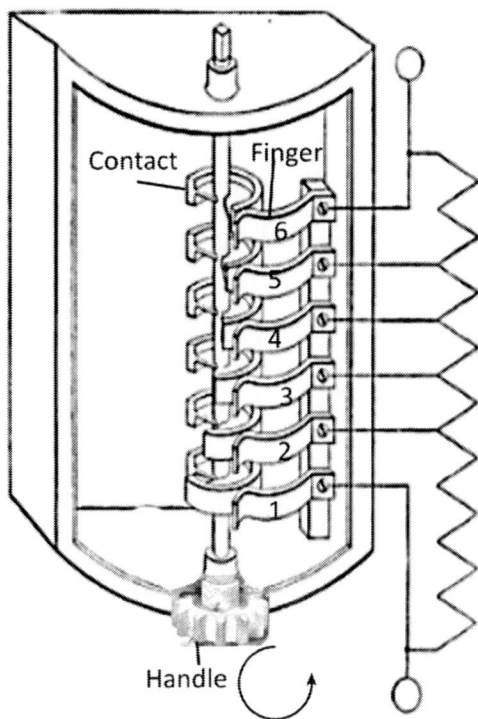

Naturally I hunted Buck up and lauded my success. Luckily for me nothing more complicated broke down that day.

I could see myself coming to like this new job. One of the things I learned right away is that a section electrician was also responsible for seeing that everything was lubricated.

Inside the control box for a cutting machine.

Consequently we had a grease gun which we had to stick into a big bucket of grease and pull the handle in order to fill the gun. Sometime later the company started buying tubes which we merely inserted into the gun, but they had a cheaper grade of grease, with a soap base.

One morning I went into the intake air course to grease the bearings of the tail piece of the pan line. It was submerged in water so I threw timbers into the water and built a sort of bridge and proceeded to grease the bearings, even though they were running in water. About an hour later I went by that tail piece and the whole area was filled with soap suds; the chain line had the same churning effect as a washing machine. Shortly after this the company went back to better-quality grease.

Early on in that mine I noticed some large, bare cables lying along the belt line and asked my cousin Walter about them. He told me they were ground wires. I knew a little about electricity by now—enough to know that to control it you must have a ground to earth somewhere, or it would find one, possibly through you—but this one stumped me. I asked Walter where these cables terminated outside. "They don't," he said.

He explained that the coal company had buried a large copper plate in the creek bed and attached a large cable to it, then buried the cable up and into the drift mouth. Everything in the mine was hooked onto this as a ground.

Again I marveled at this. Water and earth are electricity's greatest enemies and greatest friends; we were harnessing both, and just underneath our feet, and attached to nearly everything we touched.

Chapter 6 – How It's Done

Some people who have never been involved in mining have no idea how many products are derived from coal. And they have no idea of the human toil required to supply these raw materials, or that mining is not done haphazardly. In the era of hand loading men used shovels and handheld drills. Then came the cutting machine, which depended on drums and steel cables for movement and which could augur more coal in a few minutes than a man could by hand in a day.

In addition to deep mining coal is mined

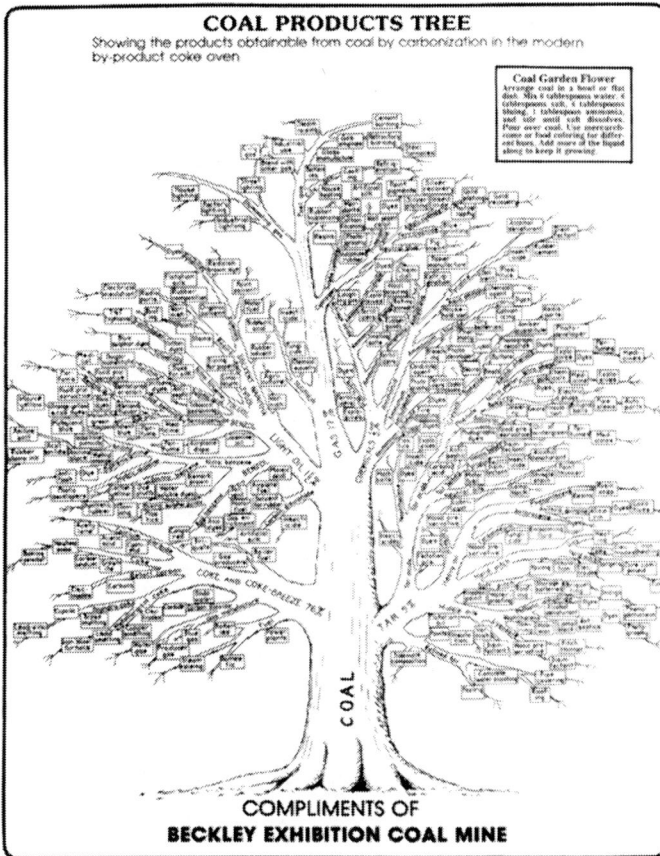

COAL PRODUCTS TREE
Showing the products obtainable from coal by carbonization in the modern by-product coke oven

Coal Garden Flower
Arrange coal in a bowl or flat dish. Mix 6 tablespoons water, 6 tablespoons salt, 6 tablespoons bluing, 1 tablespoon ammonia, and stir until salt dissolves. Pour over coal. Use mercurochrome or food coloring for different hues. Add more of the liquid along to keep it growing.

COMPLIMENTS OF
BECKLEY EXHIBITION COAL MINE

With the revolution in chemical and manufacturing processes of the 20th century, and fueled by the World War 2 need for replacements for many products derived from other sources, there seemed to be few things that couldn't be made from coal.

primarily by two methods—simply put, strip mining or its much more destructive child, mountaintop removal. I worked strictly in deep mines, which might descend as far as 10000 feet underground.

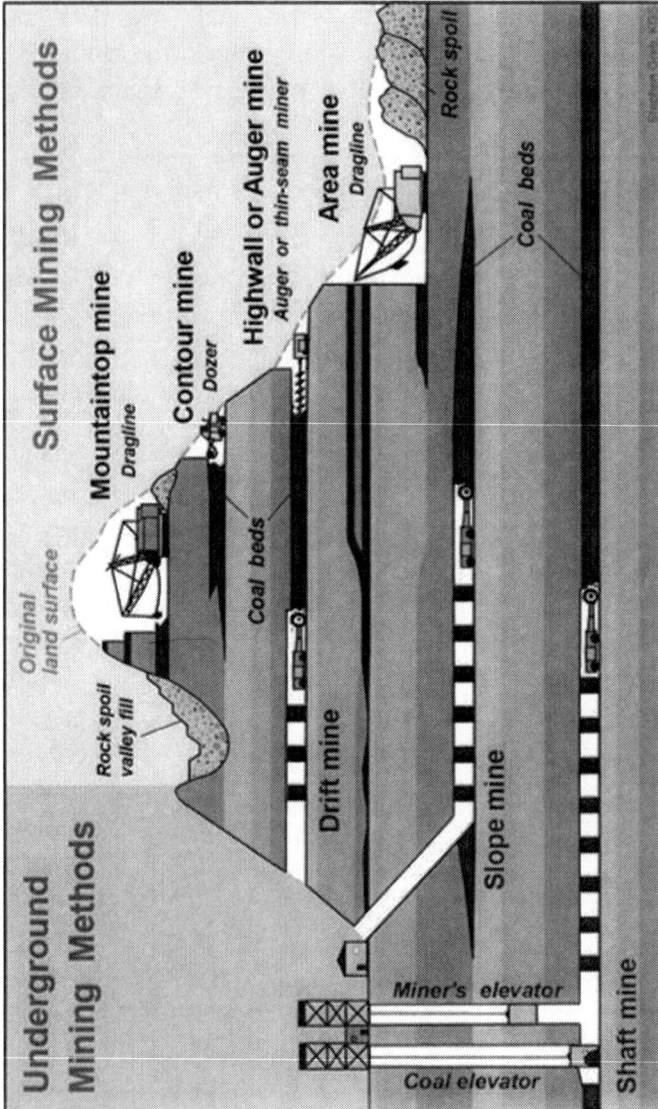

Deep mining produces a lot of refuse, when the saleable coal is separated from rock and poorer quality coal. We commonly call piles of such refuse slate dumps. These are supposed to be constantly monitored to make sure streams and neighborhoods are not damaged by runoff, which can contain heavy metals or chemicals as well as black silt which will block running streams.

Ironically, better coal processing methods meant less waste for the mine owners but also less good coal left for the taking in what they threw away.

When the Pocahontas coal company decided it wanted to timber the land around Cedar Creek, which we had leased for decades, they gave us thirty days' notice to vacate. In 1956 we moved from Otsego to the lower section of Helen, which bore the obnoxious nickname "pigpen bottom" even though any pigpens were several hundred feet south of the last house in the bottom. (Ours was the next-to-last.)

All coal mine towns were divided into "bottoms" or sections, one for whites, one for blacks, one for foreign-born, and one for bosses or foremen. The superintendent's house would be high on the hill, where he could survey the entire camp. Helen was no exception; this is just the way the towns were made. The "hollers" were named by their geographical location from the bottomland, so just below where we lived and across the railroad trestle was "first holler." A good sized stream of water flowed down from this holler and the many children who lived in the town then often were seen playing in it.

When we moved there the hills on both sides of the holler were still green and undisturbed by mining. But within a few years the coal company started mining in the upper reaches of first holler and because they did not have access to the tipple, which was a mile or so north, in third holler, they began a slate dump along the side of the holler. The coal wasn't cleaned and separated as it would be in the tipple, so a big piece of rock in the slate pile might happen to contain more coal than rock.

Thus began my habit of "gleaning" perfectly good coal that would otherwise be covered over or ignited and left to smolder to no beneficial purpose. Again, we couldn't afford to turn down free energy. This was better coal too, producing much less ash when burned than the coal we had delivered to homes by truck. That bought coal, when burned, left behind a lot of slate and rock and other material we called "clinkers," which had to be removed from our stove after every fire.

View of Helen from the Superintendent's house.

Deep mining is defined by the location of the entrance to the mine. Drift mines are placed where the coal seam can be penetrated straight into at ground level. This is the most straightforward method, whereas slope mining requires making a huge hole down to the seam, which varies in depth and usually at less than a forty-five degree angle. Small-gauge railroad tracks or beltlines are then installed from the seam up and into huge bins, resembling grain silos, and the coal is then shuttled to the preparation plant for washing and processing. Shaft mines, on the other hand, involve making an opening straight down to the coal seam.

Tipple workers first separate out rock and debris, and the coal is then passed over a series of screens of decreasing density, or grades, so coal of a certain size falls through each screen into chutes or loading booms into one of several railroad cars lined up side by side below. More modern tipples add coal washing facilities or chemical baths.

At its simplest, coal is delivered to the processing facility, known as a tipple, either by the beltline or by railroad car, then dumped into an immense hopper and carried up to the tipple by another conveyor belt. (The word "tipple" apparently derives from the fact that in some mines the railroad cars delivering coal to it were "tipped over" to dump the coal into the processing area.) The coal and other materials delivered to the tipple are "run of the mine" and contain a great deal of worthless material. Tipple workers separated out rock and debris, and these were diverted to a slack dump nearby.

I never worked in the tipple and don't personally know that much about them, but a good friend worked his entire career in tipples. John Lewis (son of Bill, an Italian immigrant miner who lived in Helen for many years and named his son after the revered

UMWA president) began working in the tipple at Helen after high school, in July 1963, and was there until 1967 when he hired on at Herndon's tipple.

His first job at Helen was to operate the "shaking table," which was part of the old tipple, but then the coal company converted to a larger screen that was actually four or five screens in one, with different size holes, all shaking at the same time. Anything larger than 3/8" was sent to another part of tipple, and separated on a big air table; fine rock would fall through into draws and to refuse, and the very fine face powder, then to "the burn." It would wring the water out, and it looked like big blobs of mud, but it was very fine coal.

The next part of the new screen system filtered out anything larger than 3/8" up to 4" and it was sent to a Daniels brand washer at the tipple. (At Helen, the Daniels washer was added in the late 50's, but the Daniels type washer is still in use today.) In such a washer magnetite (iron ore) is washed in with the coal, the magnetite making coal float and rock sink. Even in the more modern washing plants magnetite is still used, along with denatured alcohol and other chemicals. A "froth cell" takes advantage of the fact that minerals such as coal will not sink as rapidly as stone in such a liquid mix.

Slate dumps often smolder just above houses.

There were different grades and sizing for coal because different customers had different needs. For example, much of the coal from the Helen No. 10 mine was destined for Ford Motor Company's steel mills, and they would crush the coal themselves.

A Kopperston mine showing slate refuse being carried by large buckets on a tram to be dumped in the slate pile at the above right

The railroad cars acted as both storage and transportation for the coal.One car held large, more valuable lumps and others coal of decreasing size and value. Lumps that were too large to fall through the initial screens went into a crusher and were then separated by size and sent to the railroad cars. As mining modernized, more steps were added to this simple process— washing plants to remove rock and soil, centrifuges, chemical baths. Water was typically drawn from a nearby stream, and, at least before more strict mining laws, coal refuse was dumped into the same waterway, downstream. At Helen, the mine abandoned just a few years earlier was kept in use as a reservoir, filled with the water that was needed for the tipple operations. The unusable material left over after coal of various quality was sorted out was piled up nearby to form slate dumps.

At some tipples small, thin metal disks called "scatter tags" were thrown into the railroad cars to identify the mine of origin.

Another tipple job was to sample the quality of the coal, the amount that was undesirable ash after it was processed, and it was one man's job to test constantly. At least in the Helen mine the goal was about 4% ash.

Other jobs around the tipple would be to clean the railroad cars— sometimes it took all hands to clean enough for the day's run—as well as men to load the coal into the cars, run the washer, keep track of all the coal cars and the tonnage and quality of coal each carried, and so on.

One particularly dangerous job was as "dropper," the person assigned to return the coal cars to the rails after they were filled. It was all too easy to get trapped by one of the immense railroad cars. In Helen, about which more later, one mine closed down in the early 1950's and a second, tapping a different vein of coal, was built a few years later. The old mine was kept filled with water, for use in the tipple for the new mine.

The coming of strip-mining especially in the 1960's made many drift mines possible, as a hundred feet or so is gouged from the mountain, creating a high wall or cliff in the mountain—a hazard to both man and beast. Then a drift mine is cut into the mountain to retrieve the rest of the mineable coal. Recently, fracking has become prevalent and in many places its chemical refuse is a danger to the area's groundwater. It seems that the problem of waste disposal accompanies every method of excavating fossil fuels.

In a deep mine coal is separated from the surrounding rock with a cutting machine, which is typically about 28 inches high with an eight-foot cutting bar with a cutting chain, similar to a chainsaw.

One day just at quitting time a cutter chain broke on one of the machines I was responsible for. If a breakdown occurred that late the section repairman was required to stay between shifts and

B-1
MOISTURE   3.70
ASH   2.83
VOLATILE   17.25
FIXED CARBON   76.22
SULPHUR   .63
B.T.U.   14,647

Detail from an underground mine map, showing the engineers' analysis of the quality of the coal in that particular cut.

repair it for the oncoming shift. The crew was cutting pillars and consequently the top was setting up quite a rumble and I asked that one of the crew members stay and help. None agreed, leaving me alone with the broken chain, the rumble of the mountain, and worry. And fear, to be frank. The machine had toe plates on the very end held down with three-quarter inch bolts which had to be removed—chain links needed to be replaced on the end of the cutting bar.

I proceeded to pull their chain around in place but in my haste I turned one of the flanges the wrong way. I hurried and replaced the toe plates and got myself out of there into safety, to wait for the incoming crew. I heard the belt running in so I knew they were on the way. As soon as the belt cleared and reversed I crawled on it and headed home.

The next day they told me that when they started up the machine sparks flew out and the evening shift repairman had to correct it. The big laugh was when they started to cut the coal the entire cutter chain let loose with a solid ring of sparks. Heck yes, I

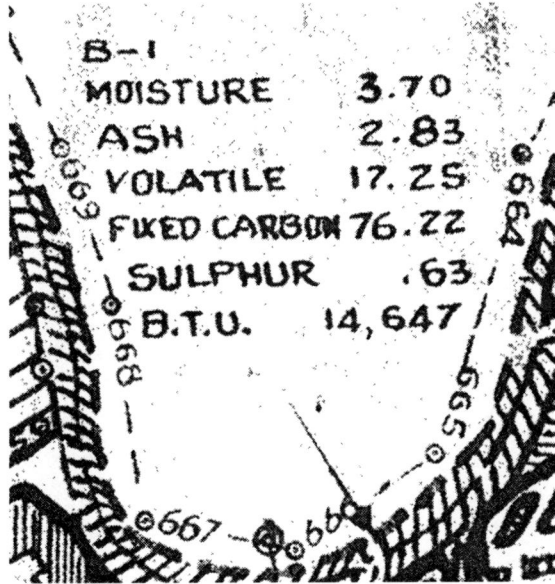

made mistakes; so does everyone who works for a living. I just chalked it up to hurry and needing to get the h—-l out of there.

This reminds me of a mistake another hoot owl repairman made when hooking up a five-horsepower motor. It was a star-wound motor with nine leads coming out of it. Leads had to be tied together—number one to number two, three to four, five to six, and so on. These were hooked to the three phases of power. 7-8-9 were tied together, insulated, and left hanging loose. This created the star pattern of a star-wound motor.

The third shift electrician was not very familiar with alternating current and he didn't know what to do with the green ground wire so he taped it up with 7-8-9. *This put 230 live volts on every bit of the face pan line, including the switch box.* When the power was plugged in the crew couldn't even get close to it—even standing nearby on the wet ground shocked them.

I knew what had happened as soon as I looked at the motor as he had wired it. I explained it to the chief electrician next time I could, just between the two of us. I was never one to sound off about another man's mistakes; I was too busy learning from (or trying to forget) my own.

There were plenty of other near-misses with high voltage. Once, for reasons unknown, a machine man's helper was crawling along with his hand wrapped around a cable when he came upon a splice which had gotten wet and he got a healthy but nonlethal shock. He yelled up at the machine man and told him he "about got prosecuted."

Grounding

Electricity requires a complete path (circuit) to continuously flow. This is why the shock received from static electricity is only a momentary jolt: the flow of electrons is

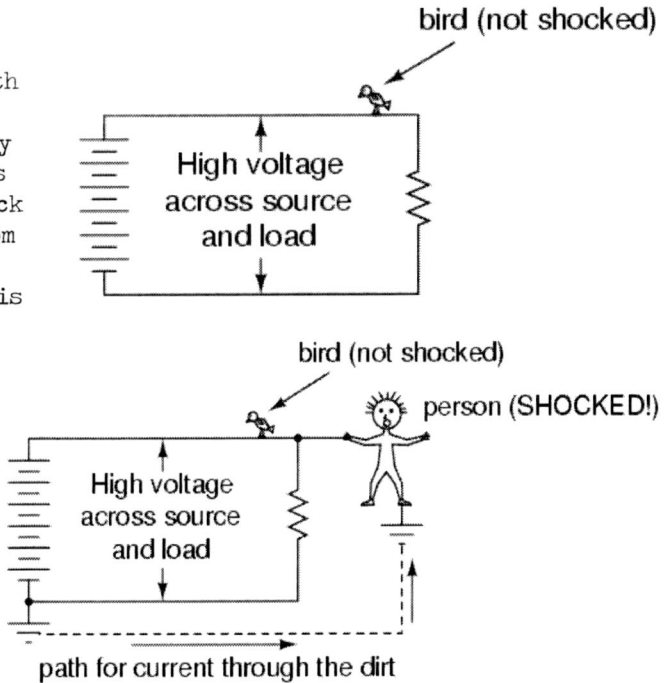

bird (not shocked)

High voltage across source and load

bird (not shocked)

person (SHOCKED!)

High voltage across source and load

path for current through the dirt

necessarily brief when static charges are equalized between two objects. Shocks of self-limited duration like this are rarely hazardous.Without two contact points on the body for current to enter and exit, respectively, there is no hazard of shock. This is why birds can safely rest on high-voltage power lines without getting shocked: they make contact with the circuit at only one point. In order for electrons to flow through a conductor, there must be a voltage present to motivate them. Voltage is *always relative between two points*. There is no such thing as voltage "on" or "at" a single point in the circuit, and so the bird contacting a single point in the above circuit has no voltage applied across its body to establish a current through it. Yes, even though they rest on *two* feet, both feet are touching the same wire, making them *electrically common*. Electrically speaking, both of the bird's feet touch the same point, hence there is no voltage between them to motivate current through the bird's body. So is it impossible to be shocked by electricity by only touching a single wire? Unfortunately, no. Unlike birds, people are usually standing on the ground when they contact a "live" wire. Many times, one side of a power system will be intentionally connected to earth ground, and so the person touching a single wire is actually making contact between two points in the circuit (the wire and earth ground).

Adapted from *Lessons In Electric Circuits* copyright (c) 2000-2015 Tony R. Kuphaldt. Used under the Design Science License.

Chapter 7 – New Paint on New Machines

One night my helper and I had to change a pump out on a cutter. There were only about three inches of clearance between the machine and roof. They drilled several holes in the top and shot out a hole in the top and trammed the cutter under it. When we got there the machine was still hot and we nearly smothered while working on it. Now and then we just dropped down on the bottom to get a good breath.

An early Jeffrey cutting machine. Its purpose is obvious from the sinister-looking augurs to the right,which could undercut a coal seam and bring down more coal in an hour than several men in a day.

I spent a lot of my time maintaining these cutting machines. Typically, a bottom cutting machine does (or did at the time) three cuts per shift. One day, well after the mid-point of the shift, the section boss crawled up and asked how many cuts they had made. The machine man answered, "When we get this one and two more it will be three." The section boss crawled to the mouth of the room, stopped suddenly and thought, what did he say? He turned around chewed out the machine man.

They were constantly improving the cutting machines, but the most popular was the Jeffrey. The Jeffrey cutter was twenty-eight inches high with an eight-foot cutting bar and could cut through pockets of sand stone.

The company I worked for began the process of installing loading machines used in conjunction with the Jeffrey cutter, which had a conveyor mounted to the pan line, consequently doing away with hand loading. The Jeffrey cutting machine had two rope drums, one on each side. One contained a half-inch cable, the other a 5/8" rope. The half-inch one was used when just pulling the machine from one place to the other, and the five-eighths was placed around pulleys and pulled out with a pipe jack hooked to it and to the roof.

When the conveyor head had to be moved the cotter pin on the half-inch drum was first removed, then the rope drum itself, and then a "cap stand" was placed onto the shaft. The cutting machine was trammed up the entry past where the conveyor head was to be mounted and the three-eighths steel cable was wrapped around the cap stand about two times and the machine was started up. When a man started pulling on the small cable the cap stand began pulling the conveyor head intact.

Once the conveyor head was moved the rope drum was replaced, the cotter pin was replaced, and we were good to go.

After the cutting, drilling and getting ready to shoot down a cut of coal, a short panline called a face conveyor would be pushed as close to the face as possible so that when the cut was shot down much of it would fill up the pans and save a lot of shoveling.

Deep mines also used coal drills. The company I worked for at that time used two kinds, the "Chicago" drill, made of copper and iron and rather heavy, and the somewhat lighter "Cincinnati" drill, made respectively by The Chicago Pneumatic Tool Company and the Cincinnati Drill Company.

The drills required a drill bit about eight feet long (the same length as the cutter bar). Five or six holes were drilled in the face of the seam of coal and filled with explosive powder and dummies tamped well into the holes. Sometimes a wire in the cable powering these drills would break and my job was to locate and correct it.

The trouble varied, as it could be a faulty switch or a bad plug-in or a short circuit. One day I found the trouble with a drill and rolled up the rest of its power cable to sit on while I made the splice. I always sang as I worked and the drill operator, Nathan Shrewsbury, was sitting there waiting and I paused my singing to tell him there was no extra charge for the singing. He had a good-natured, dry sense of humor and replied, "Well, wasn't worth much anyhow."

Another time I crawled by one man using the smaller of the drills and I noted his wet gloves and rubber boots with holes in them.

"Hey, Miller, this drills bitin' me."

"Bite it back, I advised," and kept crawling.

A Joy continuous miner.

Otsego was a coal mining town with a reputation. Makers of mining machinery learned that if a new kind of machinery needed to be tested just take it to the miners there; if they cannot mine coal with it, forget about it. The mine was owned at the time by Brule Coal Company but the miners jokingly named it Cruel Coal Company. But we were proud to have the reputation of knowing how to mine coal, and a lot of it. Coal was being mined so successfully that the foreman I worked for, at weeks end, gave each member of his crew a carton of cigarettes for each day and treated them to a dinner in Pineville—all except me. I asked him why I wasn't included. He told me I was not a part of the crew. I explained a few things about preventive maintenance and reminded him that I did a lot off it. I asked him about the small number of breakdowns he'd had.

"Dad Jim, T.I., I never thought of it like that." I was included in the celebration.

Although the coal left in pillars support the roof, they represent a lot of lost profit, as dangerous as it might be to remove them. When the Number 3 mine where I worked had driven sections back to Entry Seventeen the company decided to pull all the equipment out of Number 3 and transfer it to Number 4 , which was across on the opposite mountain. The mine foremen talked the company into pulling all the barrier pillars on the way out instead of just the equipment. This proved to be the most profitable period of mining in the seam's history.

Few readers will have heard of a "mountain ride." When a section has been driven up and the coal is mined out, the process of pulling the pillars begins, to extract the coal in the pillars supporting roof. Of course, removing the roof's support would cause the top to fall in behind the miners as they worked their way back toward the entrance to the mine. In some instances the top doesn't fall in behind; the weight of the mountain overrides the entire seam and follows the mining path, putting more and more pressure on the coal seam itself without actually caving in.

I witnessed a continuous miner sump up and start cutting across, with the helper setting timbers close to the face, about 18 inches from it. By the time the continuous miner reached halfway across the seam, thirty feet or so, the first timbers the helper set were already broken. This pressure from the mountain ride kept pushing into the seam and affected the belt entry, causing the mountain to sag down closer and closer to the belt line. It finally got so close it was dangerous to ride the belt out at quitting time. A volunteer was asked to ride out first and if he stopped and started the belt it indicated it was safe enough for the rest of us.

It got so bad that one morning we invited the superintendent to ride in with us and take a look. On reaching the working place he shut down everything, called the crews together and told them to work one continuous miner a break length (60 feet), turn 90 degrees, and start mining toward the main entries. The mountain kept up its relentless pressure while this was going on but eventually the main entry was reached and the rest of the equipment on the section, having been pulled out behind the continuous miner, reached the comparative safety of the barrier pillars.

A modern Joy cutting machine. I was often called upon to repair these, frequently starting with removing the three bolts on the front, and following the chain back to the control housing.

Earlier on, before the pullout, we had experienced another scare. Someone spotted smoke coming up the beltway. Having no idea what the source was we all headed immediately toward the air course which had been designated as the escape route.

Having been informed by the mine foreman earlier that this way was clear we headed down the air way and had gone only a few hundred feet when we came upon a rock fall. Someone shone their light under it and determined it was safe to crawl under. We had to remove our belts in order to do this.

We crawled over and under more rock falls. When we had traveled about six or seven hundred feet I decided to see if we were below the fire or above it. I took my ball peen hammer out of my belt and crawled over to the cinderblock stopping and proceeded to burst a two-inch hole in it. I stuck my mouth up close and breathed in a lung full of fresh air. I continued bursting blocks out so we could crawl out.

As we went along the belt line I spotted the source of the smoke: the light line wires had somehow gotten together and began burning through their insulation.

Meanwhile, the belt line, transformers and all the cables still had to be saved. All shifts worked around the clock. As the mechanic/electrician I always had plenty to do maintaining the equipment, splicing cables, fixing minor breakdowns and such, but in this case I worked seventeen days straight and many times doubled back on the second shift. When everything was finally in the clear and considered safe, I had already worked three straight shifts and went home, ate a sparse breakfast, and hit the sack.

No sooner did my head hit the pillow than the mine foreman wanted me to come and supervise the moving of the transformers. I begged off for a couple of hours of sleep and told him I would be there 12 o'clock sharp. He informed me I would just be supervising and asked how many men I wanted. I told him six and he said they would be there, and they were.

At that time there were always three separate transformers to move and though they were not very large they were heavy and had to be dragged to the belt line and loaded on a rack we had built for that purpose. With timbers still bending and cracking all around us, all hands worked as quickly as possible. This was a harrowing experience. Needless to say we were all much relieved when we reached the relative safety of the belthead.

The barrier pillars on each side of the main entry belt line were about four hundred feet square and on one side was a more modern miner, the Wilcox, and on the other side an old Joy Manufacturing loader. Wilcox took the Goodman cutting machine as the driver and added large augers. These augers were about twenty inches in diameter and "sump up" like a bottom machine with jacks on steel cables, which were attached to drums and then proceed to cut across the face.

A boom with conveyor chain carried the coal to the pan line. This machine only required a four man crew. Instead of having tram motors it had a drum connected to the cat chain and was controlled by pulling a brake handle; this locked one side of the loader and allowed it to maneuver left or right as called for.

The Number 3 mine had driven entries numbering up to 17 Left. This entry had also driven its depth to 2,600 feet. The coal in that entry was barely 28 inches high. Just at the time I was to catch the belt and head outside the power went off. I started crawling and went all the way outside without stopping. I bathed, went on home, ate supper and Recie and I decided to take Gil and Gloria down to Otsego to visit her parents.

When we got to their house we met a much older miner, John Meadows. He had just gotten out of the mine and by then it was about seven o'clock in the evening—it had taken him that long to crawl out of the mine. I began to realize even more clearly how quickly mining turned young men into old men.

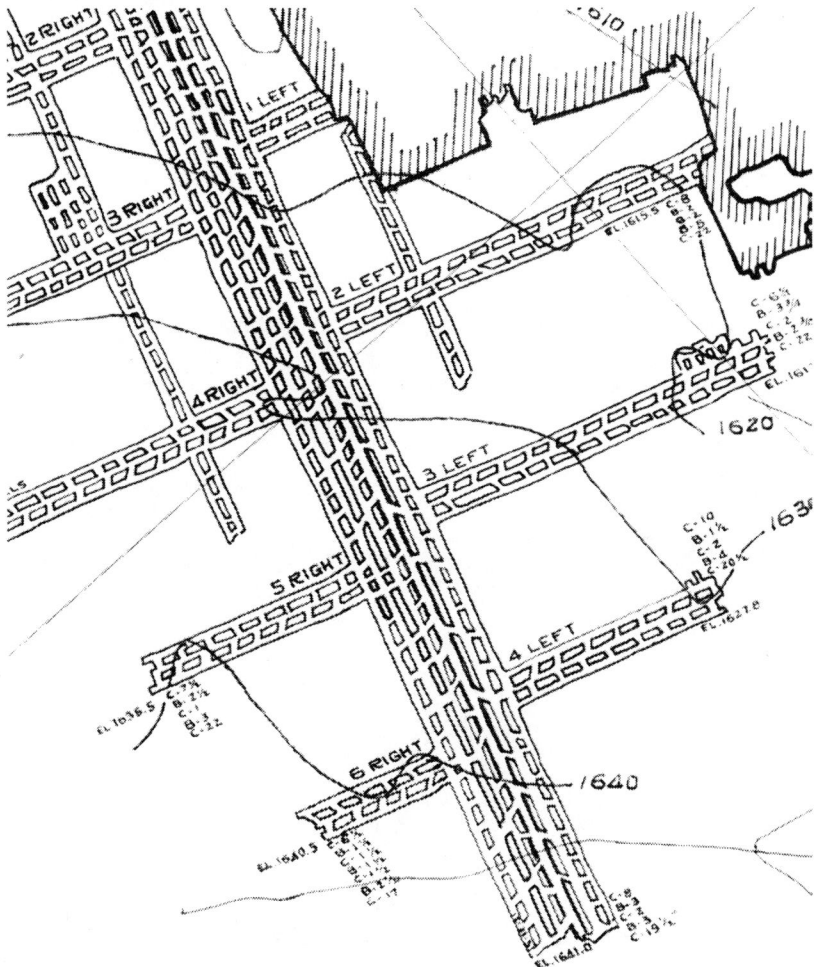

Detail of mining map showing the system of left and right sections off the mains. Note that the engineers have marked each room with details of the quality of the coal sampled from each. The perpendicular room cuts are at 60' feet each.

Mining at Number 3 soon came to an end and I was moved to Number 4. The Wilcox mining machine was in use there as well. One of the Wilcox miners had a minor breakdown and I needed only fifteen or twenty minutes to fix it. The section foreman had to account for every minute of our time so every breakdown was supposed to be recorded as to how long it took to repair. The section foreman, having had a bad run of luck for some reason, turned in forty-five minutes or an hour for my work. Next morning the mine foreman, I.P. Lambert, called me up in his office and began reading me off, wondering why it took me so long to fix this minor breakdown. Being a man of wild emotions, he took off his hard hat and slung it against the wall. It came to rest right in front of me. Meanwhile H. McKinney was watching from below and told a guy next to him.

"Watch T.I.—if he pulls his hat down on his brow he's not paying any attention to I.P."

Riding on the open man-trip, which shuttled miners to the working face and back to the surface, could be an adventure in itself; rarely would a miner be able to sit up straight for more than the first part of the journey inside.

I could not resist the temptation before me. I kicked his hat as hard as I could and it flew over and bounced off the mantrip car and rolled over the hill onto the railroad track. I turned my back to I.P. and walked down the steps with a grin on my face. Several noticed.

At Number 4 we had a short pan line dumping on the belt while the main air course pan line dumped on the short one. But when they shut down the main one the short one continued to run all day. This seemed to me a useless waste of power and unnecessary wear and tear on the equipment. I figured a way to set it so that when the main line shut down it automatically shut down the short one. I rounded up some remote cable and stretched it to the main starter of the long pan line.

Next time they shut it down I took the power off the starter, hooked the remote cable to the bottom leads, and removed the wires from the coil of the short pan line and attached the remote to the coil instead. That way when they shut down or powered on the long line it did the same for the short one. The boss came by and asked me what I was doing. I explained it to him. "Well, I'll be damned," he said. Bosses on other sections had their electricians do the same and some of them asked me what the hell I did that for. "Now I gotta do it," he grumbled. The foreman of other sections found out about it and their maintenance men came inquiring and my method was gradually adopted mine-wide.

Koppers was a very large outfit and ran the company store at Helen for many years. Notice that the picture at bottom is of the Helen store.

One Friday the company brought in a new Wilcox called the Mark 20 and I began to get a foretaste of how mechanization would change the industry. The company wanted it coal-ready by Monday morning. On Sunday night the electrician and I were told to work the hoot owl shift and double-check everything to assure immediate results when the day shift started.

That first day this one new machine mined more coal in one

shift than the old conventional mining method could in a week of double shifts.

Early in my career I would position myself where I could watch the men as they shoveled coal into the narrow pan lines. I noted there were men who were so good they could throw a shovel of coal a distance of eight feet and get every bit of it in the pan line.

But they were no match for the machines.

Mechanization resulted in many mines working out a lot more quickly and consequently the mine would shut down. This began to happen more and more frequently—when the mineable coal was exhausted the company pulled its equipment and mined out the support pillars if they could, dismantled their preparation plants, and moved on.

In the Helen mines, for instance, 950 men were employed as of 1950; but starting in the 1953 the services of hand loaders or unskilled laborers were no longer needed and the town, like so many, began its long decline in population and vitality. This left the individual coal miner and his family high and dry, with little hope unless they wanted to relocate. The miner still lived in the company house but he owned nothing. He was still required to do business with the company-owned store but by the time the company store collected his debt he sat dumbfounded and nearly broke as he considered his next move.

When the company began selling off the houses the miners lived in the miner was given the choice of buying it or staying in it only until a buyer was found; but without the prospect of working in the local mine, who could buy their own home?

I adopted the same habit of observation when I began working on the machines. I very quickly learned that if I were to be good at this I needed to start educating myself, as no one else was offering to do it for me. In fact, I tried to watch a few of the older electricians as they worked on a control box but I learned immediately that they would be of little help—they would shift their bodies around so I could not see what they were doing, lest I take their job. I was on my own.

Often I would raise the lid on a starter or other piece of equipment and just sit there and study it. I would go to the equipment supplier in Mount Hope or Oak Hill or Beckley and get a copy of the manual for some new piece of machinery, and read it closely on my own time. I learned that regardless of what machinery it was, every component had a discrete part to play on the overall machine. I began identifying each part I came in contact with, just as everything in a house has its own part to play, i.e., the refrigerator, stove, toaster and so on each have a specialty.

The amount of coal the Wilcox could mine was revolutionary, but not all the new machines were as successful. The Goodman cutting machine was a small cutter, only about 20 inches high, in use in the Beckley seam but later brought down to Number Three. This seam had little blocks of sand stone in it that caused the machine to kick back, so they discarded it.

The Joy Manufacturing Company also brought in yet another new kind of mining machine for Otsego to try out. It was huge and cumbersome, mounted on four big hydraulic jacks, designed to "walk" from face to face. The machine was raised, the huge plate moved forward, the jacks lifted, and the machine slid forward in the huge round plate. It would tram 22 feet per minute but they did not keep it very long—too many breakdowns. I was called on to work on it. One day the company sent an "expert" from Joy. He

At the bathhouse miners would raise their dirty clothes on hooks to the ceiling.

had a hose loose and told me to start the machine. I told him that was wrong but he insisted. I turned the machine on and it spewed an abundant stream of oil into his lap. I turned it off without comment. That was a hard machine to work on. For one thing, someone had to crawl into the bottom of it for maintenance—and since I was rather small, I was elected. I hated this machine and was glad when they rid themselves, and me, of it.

Some jobs I was doing were interrupted by the section foreman trying to explain that he knew a better way to do it. OK, I said, to one. It's your baby; if it doesn't work you take the blame. He just stared at me and crawled off. Another time I was adjusting a cutter chain, after having spliced it, and the section boss literally picked up some of my tools and began working on it himself. When I needed the tool he had picked up I just took it out of his hands and said in a clear voice, "I am the maintenance man, you are the foreman." That merely confirmed his place, and mine, and he left.

This may sound unbelievable but the Number 4 mine was driving in the direction of Slab Creek and consequently had to mine *under* both the creek and railroad, which ran parallel to each other. The mine engineer said that under the creek and rail line were only ten feet of cover. I soon believed this correct, for in the mine a constant stream of water and mud ran from the creek above.

When a passenger train passed overhead I could hear its rumble and feel its vibration. The mine soon dug past this crossing but as

Ohm's Law

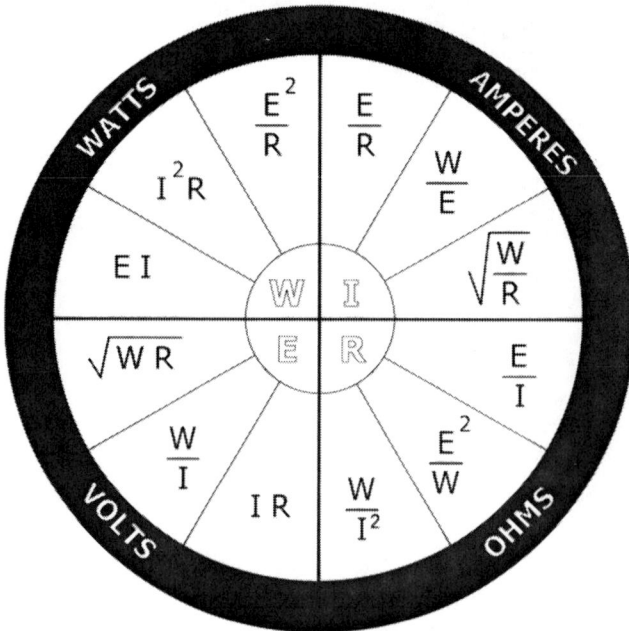

$$\frac{E^2}{R} \quad \frac{E}{R}$$
$$I^2R \quad \frac{W}{E}$$
$$EI \quad \sqrt{\frac{W}{R}}$$
$$\sqrt{WR} \quad \frac{E}{I}$$
$$\frac{W}{I} \quad \frac{E^2}{W}$$
$$IR \quad \frac{W}{I^2}$$

WATTS — AMPERES — OHMS — VOLTS

W — I — E — R

The electricity wheel, a visual representation of Ohm's law. I learned much about electricity at Coyne, but had to teach myself much more in the mines. I still have a lot to learn, of course.

the mine drove further they ran into a lot more water, eventually enough to completely cover the equipment. I was electrician/mechanic and the foreman of the section asked if I saw any sign of his mining machine. Jokingly, I told him no, I hadn't seen it, but I did spot an oil slick.

Sometimes large companies would spin off smaller "punch

mines" to replace larger mines, with the names of the owners changed in order to disengage themselves from union obligations. Local entrepreneur Tracy Hylton had such a punch mine in the beginning of his mining career. One Saturday morning he came to our home in Cedar Creek and asked me to go to his mine and check out his cutting machine. He told me my time would start when I left home and he would pay me until I finished the work and he brought me home.

The cutting machine wasn't far underground and was operated by one of my friends from high school, Charlie Brooks.

When I got there he shut the machine down. It was so hot I couldn't touch it with my bare hands. Fortunately I had picked up a pair of gloves before leaving home.

At the time I had no experience with direct current power—which is more efficient in some high-voltage distribution scenarios—so approached it cautiously. But I carried my ohmmeter at all times and while others would be working on something else I would take the cover off a machine's control box and check the voltage on whatever it was. When I had removed all the bolts and looked at the fingers and "segments," or contact points for the fingers, I saw the trouble immediately.

This machine's four-step system was made so the first contact went through the resistance and the remaining three, as they made contact through to the fourth, put the machine across the line, meaning the resistance was bypassed and full voltage was applied. The electrical components had four contacts and I saw it made contact with only the first one. This told me the operator had been running the machine through the resistance.

I set about adjusting the fingers and testing each to see that they made proper sequential contact. I told Mr. Hylton I could not guarantee how long the machine would last since all the windings had been subjected to extreme heat. He understood and paid me for my time and dropped me off back at home. If you do something once, people tend to believe you know what you're doing and expect you to be able to do it again. Do it enough and you might even convince yourself.

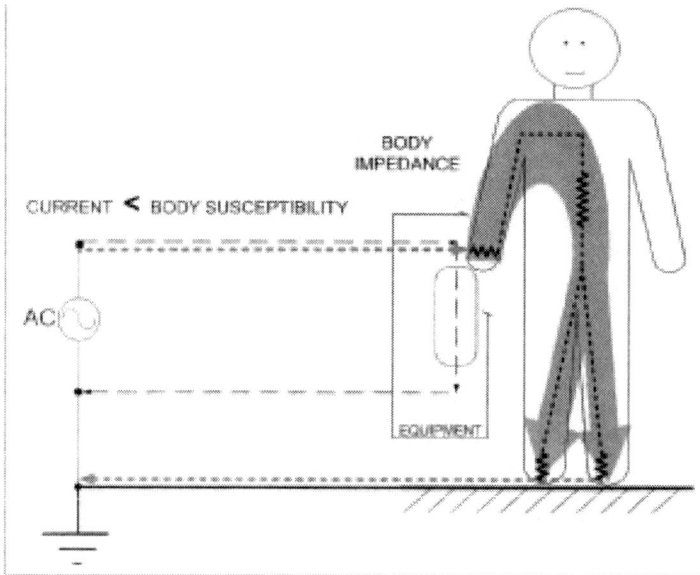

Physiological effects of electricity

As electric current is conducted through a material, any opposition to that flow of electrons (resistance) results in a dissipation of energy, usually in the form of heat. This is the most basic and easy-to-understand effect of electricity on living tissue: current makes it heat up. If the amount of heat generated is sufficient, the tissue may be burnt. The effect is physiologically the same as damage caused by an open flame or other high-temperature source of heat, except that electricity has the ability to burn tissue well beneath the skin of a victim, even burning internal organs.

Another effect of electric current on the body, perhaps the most significant in terms of hazard, regards the nervous system. By "nervous system" I mean the network of special cells in the body called "nerve cells" or "neurons" which process and conduct the multitude of signals responsible for regulation of many body functions. The brain, spinal cord, and sensory/motor organs in the body function together to allow it to sense, move, respond, think, and remember.

Nerve cells communicate to each other by acting as "transducers:" creating electrical signals (very small voltages and currents) in response to the input of certain chemical compounds called *neurotransmitters*, and releasing neurotransmitters when stimulated by electrical signals. If electric current of sufficient magnitude is conducted through a living creature (human or otherwise), its effect will be to override the tiny electrical impulses normally generated by the neurons, overloading the nervous system and preventing both reflex and volitional signals from being able to actuate muscles. Muscles triggered by an external (shock) current will involuntarily contract, and there's nothing the victim can do about it.

This problem is especially dangerous if the victim contacts an energized conductor with his or her hands. The forearm muscles responsible for bending fingers tend to be better developed than those muscles responsible for extending fingers, and so if both sets of muscles try to contract because of an electric current conducted through the person's arm, the "bending" muscles will win, clenching the fingers into a fist. If the conductor delivering current to the victim faces the palm of his or her hand, this clenching action will force the hand to grasp the wire firmly, thus worsening the situation by securing excellent contact with the wire. The victim will be completely unable to let go of the wire.

Medically, this condition of involuntary muscle contraction is called *tetanus*. Electricians familiar with this effect of electric shock often refer to an immobilized victim of electric shock as being "froze on the circuit." Shock-induced tetanus can only be interrupted by stopping the current through the victim.

Even when the current is stopped, the victim may not regain voluntary control over their muscles for a while, as the neurotransmitter chemistry has been thrown into disarray. This principle has been applied in "stun gun" devices such as Tasers, which on the principle of momentarily shocking a victim with a high-voltage pulse delivered between two electrodes.

The diaphragm muscle controlling the lungs, and the heart – which is a muscle in itself – can also be "frozen" in a state of tetanus by electric current. Even currents too low to induce tetanus are often able to scramble nerve cell signals enough that the heart cannot beat properly, sending the heart into a condition known as *fibrillation*. A fibrillating heart flutters rather than beats, and is ineffective at pumping blood to vital organs in the body. In any case, death from asphyxiation and/or cardiac arrest will surely result from a strong enough electric current through the body. Ironically, medical personnel use a strong jolt of electric current applied across the chest of a victim to "jump start" a fibrillating heart into a normal beating pattern.

That last detail leads us into another hazard of electric shock, this one peculiar to public power systems. Though our initial study of electric circuits will focus almost exclusively on DC (Direct Current, or electricity that moves in a continuous direction in a circuit), modern power systems utilize alternating current, or AC. The technical reasons for this preference of AC over DC in power systems are irrelevant to this discussion, but the special hazards of each kind of electrical power are very important to the topic of safety.

How AC affects the body depends largely on frequency. Low-frequency (50- to 60-Hz) AC is used in US (60 Hz) and European (50 Hz) households; it can be more dangerous than high-frequency AC and is 3 to 5 times more dangerous than DC of the same voltage and amperage. Low-frequency AC produces extended muscle contraction (tetany), which may freeze the hand to the current's source, prolonging exposure. DC is most likely to cause a single convulsive contraction, which often forces the victim away from the current's source.

AC's alternating nature has a greater tendency to throw the heart's pacemaker neurons into a condition of fibrillation, whereas DC tends to just make the heart stand still.

Chapter 8 – Famous Miners I Have Known

The chapter title is obviously ironic; the lives of men and women of my generation were often marked only by a census taker and eventually a small stone in a family cemetery, if they were lucky. Ironically, the men whom I knew that died in the mines probably achieved their greatest chance at being remembered by the simple act of dying underground. The mine became their tomb, and their name finally appeared in a local newspaper. The hills around my hometown of Otsego and around Helen are really burial mounds.

Although the towns themselves were segregated, though with a lot of overlap because they were so small, the mines themselves were not. Black, white, and foreign miners worked alongside each other with very little racial or ethnic problems, mainly because we were all in it together, a thousand feet underground doing hard, dangerous and dirty work. You respected a man for his work ethic, not his color or language. Too, mining companies were chronically short of laborers and so would place ads around the world to try and attract steady workers.

Between 1880 and my birth in 1919 the population of southern West Virginia exploded from 93,000 to an astounding 446,000, according to the Coal Heritage Authority, due entirely to the expansion of coal mining in the area. This meant that coal mine operators needed men, and plenty of them. If a man could mine coal, the company did not particularly care about his ethnicity or color.

I always found it strange that although we were all black by the time our shift ended we would retreat to our own neighborhoods, with the white miners getting marginally better homes. And we were all overseen by the Super, looking down from his fancy perch.

As in any industry, mining had its own eccentrics, but perhaps the constant danger in the mine produced more than its share. I worked the evening shift with an older man nicknamed "Shakedown." Someone brought out a roll of canvas and leaned it against the wall. Along comes Shakedown with an ax, which he stuck in the canvas, thinking, I guess, it was a timber. The evening shift boss fired him. Shakedown said, "You can't fire me." He went home but the next morning he simply showed up on the day shift and got a brush hook and started cutting weeds. He more or less came and went as he pleased and did whatever he wanted to do without anyone questioning him.

One night the rock dust crew came out and announced they were going to start dusting the Number 8 East entry at a certain time. That entry had a double-stopping about eight feet apart in accordance with the ventilation system. We left and went elsewhere to finish the shift and missed one of our crew. We had not seen him since we left and on the way out someone decided to look for him. They found him asleep between the stoppings and completely white with rock dust. He blended in so well with his surroundings he was almost invisible. His eyes had been shut and the rock dust had filled even the hollows of his eyes. He looked just like a ghost.

I still have that lunch bucket.

I also became friends with an Italian man named Jim Lamboni. He was about 5'2" and his American wife Irene, a widow with the married name of Stevenson, was much taller. She and Jim were well respected and liked throughout the town. I came to know Jim well and he was an amusing man. In a previous accident he had lost his thumb and forefinger. He never learned to pronounce my name so just yelled "hey Firmer!" He yelled at me one day to say his "no fumb" was hurting. Jim and I had bucket buckets exactly alike, the silver, rounded type many miners used.

One morning I had to go in early so just grabbed up a lunch pail and hit the belt. Jim always had his wife pack a lot of pepperoni and spicy sandwiches in his. On the other hand, because my system was so beaten down by malaria, my lunch consisted of just one apple butter sandwich, an oatmeal cake and a small jar of skim milk. When dinnertime arrived the phone rang. "Hey Firmer, Hey Firmer, I think a'we traded a buckets!" He looked at mine in a panic. Jim's job was to take care of the belt so I knew he was near the other end of it from where I was, so I got hold of the guy at the belthead and had him watch and I transferred Jim's dinner down to him on the beltline. Had I downed Jim's spicy food I would have ended up in the hospital.

The Otsego chief, my first cousin Walter Sizemore, asked me to come back to Otsego. I told him I would for day shift. He said OK. On Saturday evening I went to the bath house to confirm coming back and he told me to come out on the second shift, which I hated. I reminded him of his promise and told him I still had my job at Tralee and would not work the second shift. He said he had changed his mind and told me to come out on the night shift. I told him no, I still have a job at Tralee if I want it. Well then, he said, come out on the day shift on Monday.

Walter's mother, Julie Rinehart Sizemore, was my mother's sister. But being related to the chief did not mean I was favored. One day as I was crawling up toward the face I passed a man shoveling coal on the pan line. I stopped and we chatted a spell and he asked me how I got my job. He told me he had four years college. He asked about who the chief was and when I told him he was my cousin. "Oh, so that's how you got that easy job." No, I told him, a man named Cecil Fulmer was chief and he's the one who hired me.

Walter was as smart as any boss I ever worked for. He could solve problems beyond anyone else. Once, a belt greaser, Russell Odell was electrocuted. Experts were called in to examine all aspects of the tragedy. They were assembled in a room with the company officials, including Walter.

The electrical engineers all drew their opinions on the blackboard as to how this man had been killed. Walter took it all in but remained silent during their discourses.

When they were all finished he went up to the blackboard and drew a simple diagram demonstrating the exact way the accident occurred. His explanation was simple and to the point. The mine was then run on three separate transformers, with the primary side at 2300 volts and secondary at 240 volts. A small piece of rock had fallen on the primary side and pushed the ground wire down on one phase of the transformer. This in turn placed high voltage on all of the ground wires throughout. As the belt greaser started his job there was a belt pan lying on both the ground wire and the belt system. When the greaser put his grease gun on a fitting on one of the rollers he connected with the high voltage. One of the engineers said there went his college degree down the drain.

It was hard to lose friends, but death and disability were a

ia) • 17 Dec 1965, Fri • Page 1

Wyoming Men Hurt By Mine Gas Blast

OTSEGO (RNS) — Two Wyoming County men were injured at about noon Thursday at the Oglebay Norton Co. mine here.

A relative of one of the injured men quoted the man as saying a spark from machinery set off a gas explosion in the mine.

Mine officials refused to comment.

Lloyd Thomas Kellam of Ravencliff is a patient at the Wyoming General Hospital at Mullens where he is being treated for burns over 50 per cent of his body. His condition was listed as serious.

Kester D. Green of Otsego, who received second and third degree burns on his arms, hands and face, is a patient in Bluefield Sanitarium. His condition was listed as satisfactory.

constant reminder that we were extracting valuable energy from the earth in the most unforgiving circumstances. Sometimes it was just a moment of inattention.

In early December 1965 I helped Tom Kellam fill out his retirement papers. He was to work his last day on December 16. He was looking forward to it. He packed his lunch that day and kissed his wife goodbye, not knowing that it would be not only his last day as a miner, but his last of conscious living.

Tom was a pumper and he and foreman Kester Green went down into an abandoned portion of the mine to check on the water there. Their motor had to go through swag with a foot or so of water standing in it. When they came to the swag they just dropped the pole that energized the small locomotive they were riding. Instead of turning the controller off, they dropped the pole and let their momentum propel them to the other side of the water.

When they lifted the pole back up to reapply power to the locomotive it sparked a pocket of methane gas, which naturally gathered at the higher part of the roof. Green had one ear burned off and his face was burned very badly. Tom was

Wyoming Miner Killed By Slate

PINEVILLE, May 2 — Funeral services are to be conducted in Alabama for Coy Cordar, 32, of Mullensville, who was killed about 8 o'clock last night when he was pinned beneath a timber in a slate fall at the Wyoming mine of the Red Jacket Coal Corporation.

His body is to be shipped to Birmingham, Ala., with burial to be held in the Liberty Cemetery at Dixiana, Ala.

Superintendent D. L. Haga said the fatal accident was the first in the Wyoming mine in more than four years. Cordar, employed for about a year and a half as a cutting machine operator, was found in a jackknifed position with his right knee up to his chest. He is believed to have smothered or suffered a broken neck in the accident.

also badly burned and went into a coma, surviving in that condition for thirty days before he passed away. I couldn't help but think of the ironies of the war I fought, as young men lost their lives just because they were a few inches left or right of a bullet.

In the early days of hand loading in small cars the miners used carbide lamps, which had an open flame on them. Since these early mines were not very deep the danger of methane was small but sometimes it would gather and be sparked by any small flame. Since methane gathered near the top the miners would lie down flat on the bottom and push their lamps up into the top and the open flame would set off a small explosion, which the miners merely described as "burning out the work place."

The Number 3 seam where I was working was a gassy mine. By this time the Jeffrey bottom machines had been replaced with Wilcox miners. Made just up the road in Oak Hill, West Virginia, the Wilcox miners were made from old Goodman bottom machines but equipped with twenty-four inch augers. These augers had a lot of cutting bits, the same kind of bits used in the Jeffrey cutters. These had a set screw so they could be replaced as necessary. The bits fit into a mountain lug, which sometimes broke off and had to be welded back on. I was not a certified welder but most repairmen just picked up the skills they needed by observation and practice.

The miner was cutting on an upgrade and consequently was prone to gathering methane gas, and since the gas was lighter than air it gathered at the highest point. I asked the foreman before I struck an arc to make a weld whether he had taken a gas test. He just laughed and said there was no gas. I insisted that a gas check be taken, and was well within my rights. He tested for gas and it turned out the area was full of gas. I insisted that canvas be rigged all the way to where I was to weld. This could have been a disaster. It always paid to check for gas.

At Herndon the company came up with an idea of creating a greaser crew, with the responsibility to lubricate all the machinery. They were each issued a grease gun. One morning on the way outside on the man trip cars three of us were sitting on one side. I was on the right and I noticed the man in the middle had inserted the end of his grease gun into the jacket pocket of the man beside him. He was pumping the handle up and down, filling the man's jacket pocket full of grease. I got off before them so never saw his response, but I'm sure it was entertaining.

As it is with war so it is with work—days of stress and fear are made bearable only by moments when laughter. One of my friends also worked the hoot owl shift but when the man-trip came to the surface I noticed he was not on it. Knowing the guy, when the man trip let us off at my entry I made a hasty trip by all the conveyor heads and finally found him sound asleep. He uttered only two words: "bat shit." I took his ball-peen hammer and made a few loud noises as if we were just finishing a repair job. A neat cover-up. He just put on his hard-top hat and left for the surface.

The laughter sometimes came at each other's expense. One Monday morning I got ready to go to work and had worn a white shirt on Sunday. Recie said she was not going to wash clothes that day so I just kept the white shirt on and went to work. In the bathhouse another miner took a look at me and said, "Wow, look at old T.I., he sure dresses up to come to work." I just laughed and passed it off.

In a while he mentioned it again, then several more times. I called out his name very loudly and told him some day someone was going to stick a pin in him and let all that hot air out and he would fly around the room like a big balloon. The bathhouse roared and his face got a sickly shade of pink.   One day up on the railroad tracks a couple of bosses were joking around and one said he had heart burn. Another offered him an Alka-Seltzer.

"I wonder what it would be like to swallow one without water?" he said.

He did and got it stuck in his throat. He could still breathe but drank a gallon of water before it dissolved.

One morning we all happened to get outside several minutes before quitting time. I walked over and began pushing hard on a cinder block wall. The boss asked what the heck I was doing that for. "I'm standing in a strain until quitting time," I said.

Chapter 9 – Catching a Breath

Tragedy is never far from the minds of any family who lives near a coal mine. Seventy-five years ago a pocket of gas exploded in the Otsego mine, resulting in the death of two brothers and two other men. Stanley Ray and Bruce Ray, both of Hotchkiss, died. Stanley was just 24 and a recent bridegroom. His brother, Bruce, was only 30. The explosion also took John Mullins of Clay and Joe Hooper of Beckley, 32. When these incidents occur it's always an injury to the community as a whole; the entire population becomes family. Jim Lamboni was also seriously injured in a slate fall, and was confined thereafter to the Wylie Hospital of Mullens with a broken back.

During the first decade of the 1900's there were several mine explosions which resulted in the appointment of officials from the federal Department of Mines to insure proper mining methods were employed, and rescue training became an important part of mining, even to the present.

I have been witness to many accidents in my tenure as miner. Being an electrician/mechanic I could roam among all the miners on the section where I worked and I carried a small medical kit with me and took care of lots of minor injuries, mostly on the spot and without interrupting the mining.

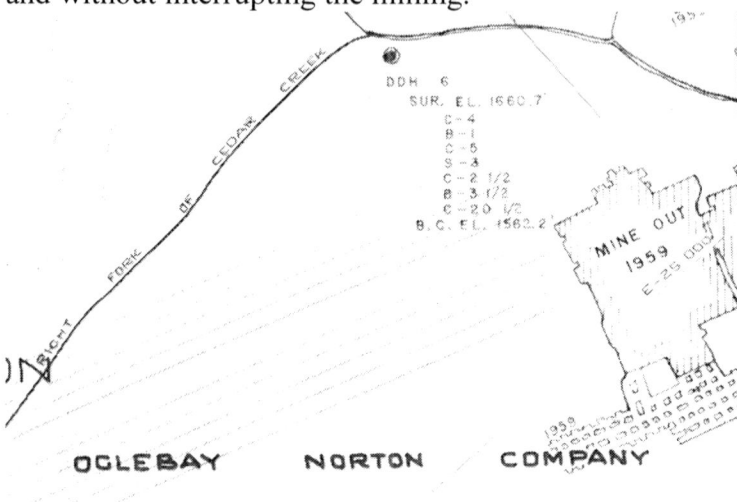

At ten o'clock Tuesday morning, October 29, 1958 there was a huge explosion at the Oglebay-Norton mine near Craigsville.

Oglebay-Norton, my employer at the time, was a large outfit. "The company that would become Oglebay Norton was established in 1851 and quickly moved into the growing iron-ore market. In 1855, it employed then-unknown John D. Rockefeller as a bookkeeper at $3.50 a week... Decades of high demand for steel — fueled by the rise of the automobile and two world wars — kept the company busy, as did forays into coal and taconite... In 1957, it absorbed some of its affiliates, adopted the name Oglebay Norton Company, and began trading publicly... Oglebay's most famous brush with unwanted attention came with the sinking of the Edmund Fitzgerald amid freakishly bad weather on Lake Superior in 1975."[3]

Rites Set Today For Mine Victim

MULLENS, Oct. 30 (RNS) — Funeral services for Olen C. Gates, 50, who was killed in an explosion Tuesday at the Oglebay-Norton Co. Mine at Summersville will be conducted at 3 p.m. Friday in Sanford, N. C., with burial to follow there.

Gates, who was superintendent of the mine, was one of 13 killed in the explosion.

Gates formerly was employed as superintendent of the Otsego Mine of the Brule Smokeless Coal Co., a subsidiary of the Oglebay-Norton Co.

At the Oglebay explosion Percy Bright, whom I also knew from Otsego, came in and began preparing coffee and sandwiches to be brought in for the gathering family members awaiting news of their loved one. A troubled family people will find their way to a disaster; no power can stop them from asking the ultimate question: *Is my husband OK? Is my son hurt?*

Conversely, at least when mining was a more human-driven

---

[3] *http://www.clevescene.com/cleveland/the-wreck-of-the-oglebay-norton/Content?oid=1487868*

occupation, almost no amount of preparation or expense seemed capable of preventing Earth's fury from unleashing where it would. The November 29, 1954 edition of Life magazine featured a story entitled, a little clumsily, "Death's Mask at a Coal Pit," detailing the death of fifteen men at a Farmington mine; it was a model mine, and the union and company both presumed it was state-of-the-art in terms of safety.

The "several million dollars" the company expended to make it a model mine could not prevent Jamison Coal's No. 9 mine become a vast sealed tomb for those fifteen unfortunates.

Among the dead were two men I knew well, Olen Gates, who had been Superintendent at Otsego, and Edward Stevenson, his assistant. I grew up with the latter—we were in grade school together. Edward was just 38, and was the son of Irene Stevenson, Jim Lamboni's wife, Irene, who had passed on in 1953 at just fifty years of age. Among those waiting was Goldie Hinkle, whom I also knew from Otsego. I had talked with her family many times. Comfort was offered even where misery would not cease.

Olen Gates' wife arrived, ready to support her husband in his terrible responsibility; but Olen was already dead, and she collapsed on learning of his fate. Gates was killed by black damp, a mixture of carbon dioxide and nitrogen (though the term is also applied to an atmosphere depleted of oxygen, rather than having an excess of carbon dioxide).

Fifty men went in to work, and only thirty-one came out. The headline in the October 29, 1958 Daily Times of New Philadelphia, Ohio, blared "Victims of Mine Blast Leave Total of 47 Dependents." (As is typical of mine blasts, over and over, just below the headline there appears a first-person account of a miner who had survived a similar explosion.)

Where a mine was located near a town, it would not be unusual for miners' families to envision them working away every day half a mile directly beneath their feet, or beneath the furniture store or high school; and indeed, in this particular explosion, one of the miners who managed to get out noted of the potential survivors that, "If they are trapped. They are about right under Dr. David Brown's office, I'd say about two miles under the mountain. Maybe less."

The first-person account of the Craigsville disaster from the

October 29, 1958, Richwood (WV) *News Leader* ends only a little more poetically than these disaster stories always end: "The 13th and the last stretcher burden is brought forth from the earth. Four men carry it to the locker room and lay it there, and again I witness the unhurried dread, the hoped for avoidance of a job that must be done, and the thongs are cut and the blankets lowered and identity has been established. And a chapter has been written with a pen dipped in abject sorrow... I have walked out in the street and find no laughter. The town and its people weep because in our little sphere of things we don't live to ourselves alone. Our greatest tragedy has crushed us all."

Each mining career of substantial length is a diary of near-misses. On one of the sections I worked there was a big slate fall, which covered a loading machine. It would not run and the evening shift had determined the trouble was in the starting box. When I got to the machine I noted it was completely covered with the fallen rock. But the roof was unstable; how long would it hold? Yet I was being paid—and good wages for the time and place, at that—to rescue this machine.

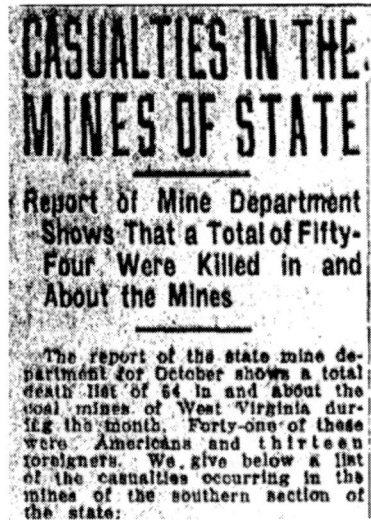

CASUALTIES IN THE MINES OF STATE

Report of Mine Department Shows That a Total of Fifty-Four Were Killed in and About the Mines

The report of the state mine department for October shows a total death list of 54 in and about the coal mines of West Virginia during the month. Forty-one of these were Americans and thirteen foreigners. We give below a list of the casualties occurring in the mines of the southern section of the state:

A headline from a West Virginia paper in the 1930's. The most remarkable thing about it is how unremarkable it was that fifty-four men died that month.

On the side where the starting box was I found a crawlspace just high enough for me to crawl into. Another huge rock lay at an angle and I had to lie on my side just to remove the bolts. After finally getting the lid off I found the trouble and fixed it as quickly as possible. I hurriedly replaced the lid and backed myself out.

Even in my childhood in the twenties I recall mining accidents that produced tragic results. The railroad tunnel at Otsego was constructed wide enough to accommodate double tracks, which for some reason were never built. Pedestrians traveling through the tunnel would sometimes be confronted by an oncoming fast train. In those days big coal-burning Mallet (pronounced *malley*) locomotives plied the tracks and emitted a lot of smoke. The wide part of the tunnel provided space to hover low to avoid the smoke, but there were no guarantees. One man was found dead in the tunnel but exactly what killed him will never be known.

One occupation at the tipple was commonly referred to as the "car dropper." A "car dropper" is responsible for manning loaded railroad cars and letting them "drop" by gravity away from the tipple and off to a side track, awaiting their turn to be added to other cars and shipped out by the railroad. A man by the name of Poe had this job when I was at Otsego.

One day he mounted a loaded railroad car, loosened the brake and let it start a slow drift down-track. He—or someone, it was never clear—had failed to throw the switch which would have let the car follow a straight track to its destination. Another railroad car was parked just at the switch and his car hit the parked one corner to corner. He evidently wasn't watching and the corners of

MINE LOCOMOTIVE AND DRIFT
MOUTH AT KAY MOOR, W. VA.

A typical small mine locomotive. Electricity is applied via the pole that hangs at right by touching it to the high-voltage wire strung all through the mine.

the two cars pinned his body between them. His chest and stomach were crushed but he was alive, barely.

The men gathered around him but he told them not to release

him until he had told them his last wishes; he knew he would die when the cars were separated.

A mine typically uses a tram line, with shallow bucket-like pans loaded with coal refuse and mounted on wire ropes. The loaded cars were pulled to the top, emptied, and returned to the tipple. On returning, the buckets had to rotate around a pulley-like machine with a six-inch clearance between the ropes and bucket. One day the man operating it accidentally fell upon the ropes and his body was carried through the six-inch opening, killing him instantly.

The belt line, which carried both men and coal deep into the mountain, was equally dangerous. I often had to maintain belt feeders. These were located over the end of the belt and the feeder had its own conveyor chain so that when a buggy full of coal was dumped on it started automatically. The buggy man dumped his load onto the feeder and left, and when the last of the coal dumped on the belt the feeder stopped automatically. Sometimes a man would attempt to change a roller while the belt was running full of coal, resulting in the belt catching the arm and cutting it off. I personally knew two men killed in this job, Dasil Sizemore and Ralph Halsey. Another, Elva Bird, permanently damaged his hand and wrist and nearly lost his arm.

Accidents happen so quickly. Once, I was helping to remove a belt structure, which put me in line to pass an eight-foot angle iron on to the next man. I accidentally let it slide across just above my knee. The knee swelled up to twice its size. The doctor inserted a large needle and extracted bloody liquid from my knee. He told me that somewhere in the distant future this would give a lot of trouble. True enough, this came to pass in 1994 when I had to have the knee replaced.

Methane—a highly flammable, naturally occurring gas—is another constant danger in coal mining. Because of the risk of methane, any ventilation equipment had to be carefully installed and monitored on a regular basis. The company I worked for at the time had an immense ventilation fan located at the mouth of an old entryway as a part of the exhaust system.

One day it was discovered that a large pillow block bearing on the exhaust fan was overheating. Replacing it was scheduled for a Saturday. The Super came asked me to help with it. When we got to it he looked at the other mechanic and said about me, "I got him as a last resort." I marked these words and from then on had little opinion of him. I helped get the bearing off, a very large bearing with a four-inch opening, resembling in shape a tambour clock, shaped like a bell curve.

We built a large fire and filled a large container with kerosene. When it began to boil we put the huge new bearing into the oil; it had to be boiled for at least two hours in order for it to expand enough to slip onto the shaft in one smooth movement, then shrinking in place as it cooled.

One night I was working on a loader and had to change out a conveyor motor. It was a small motor, not seventy pounds, and set on an angle. I had the motor sitting on some half headers (two inches by eight by twenty inches long) and almost had the motor ready to apply power and engage it with the reduction housing. I was just pulling my hand out from between the motor and housing when it slipped into place very quickly.

I jerked the forefinger on my left hand loose and looked at it. The end of my finger was hanging over and was cut all the way around both sides of my fingernail. I saw the bone exposed so I placed my finger into my right palm and gently pushed it back over the bone. I took a clean cloth out of my coveralls and bandaged it up.

I started crawling out to the belt line and came outside, bathed, and drove myself to the hospital where a Chinese doctor sewed up the end of it. Next day the mine superintendent read me off good and told me to never do that again—that is, drive myself to the hospital. I hoped it wouldn't be a common occurrence.

One time on the 17 Left section the power suddenly went off. It was early in the shift and normal troubleshooting failed to find the trouble. The suspect was the high voltage cable feeding the transformers but just crawling along the length of the cable and visually inspecting it failed to reveal the problem. A helper and I started at the oil switch and began to wipe down every foot of the cable.

After hand-wiping six or seven hundred feet of the cable I found what I was looking for: a brown spot about the size of a

DATE	16	17	18	19	20	21	22	23	24	25	26	27	28	29	30	31	TOTAL HOURS	TOTAL AMOUNT
REG. HRS.				8	8	8	8	8		8	8	8						
REG. AMT.																		229.44
O.T. HRS.		8							16									
O.T. AMT.		16.00			5.38				8.45									137.54

					TOTAL GROSS EARNINGS →	364.84
OGLEBAY NORTON COMPANY				OTHER DEDUCTIONS	AMOUNT
BRULE MINE				OPEN ACCOUNT	
INDIVIDUAL TIME AND PAYROLL				RENT	
SUMMARY				COAL	
				W. VA. SALES TAX	
				DOCTOR	4.00
NAME, NUMBER, AND PAY PERIOD ENDING				UNION—U. M. W. OF A.	5.50
				BURIAL/WELFARE FUND	5.00
				DONATIONS	
2081 - T. I. Miller - 2				TOOLS	
				SUPPLIES	
Jan. 15, 1965				INSURANCE	6.70
				GARNISHEE	
				GARNISHEE FEE	
				SUNDRY	
				TOTAL OTHER DEDUCTIONS	21.70

GROSS EARNINGS		DEDUCTIONS				AMOUNT DUE EMPLOYEE	CHECK NO.
	TOTAL	W. H. TAX	F.I.C.A.	STATE TAX	OTHER		
	364.84	44.60	13.14	3.70	21.70	281.74	2989

My pay stub from Oglebay Norton, 1965, with deductions for doctor, union dues, and so on.

nickel. I mashed it with my thumb. It was soft and spongy. I knew I had found the trouble. I skinned about a foot of the cable with my knife and found that one phase, one cable encased in the rubberized shielding, had contacted the ground wire. I separated the wires and taped them up properly and called to the belt head for the person there to turn on the oil switch. Power was restored and the problem solved.

The next Saturday Conley and I were delegated to make a permanent splice in the cable. I told him to wear his coat; he didn't. I had mine on and was still cold so I just told him to find some place warm and wait for me. I was almost finished anyhow. These splices were to be done a certain way and I could do them quickly, but to do them right I could only do two in a single shift.

One Saturday I was detailed to take out an illegal high-voltage wiring splice about eight feet from a bank of transformers. Upon arrival at the mouth of the section I pulled the oil switch, removed all three disconnects and placed them on the locomotive I was using, all according to company rules. This, in effect, was supposed to remove all power from the transformers. But when I reached the transformers they were still powered on, the pump was running and the lights still burning. Why? Hadn't I pulled the switch, removed the disconnects?

This was a dangerous situation and I wanted no part of it. I reversed the motor and went back to the mouth to make sure someone had not put an illegal jumper around the switch. Finding none I called the Superintendent. He first told me I was crazy. I replied, "I may be crazy but I ain't stupid."

He called the chief and both came in to confirm what I had seen. The chief said he knew what the trouble was. On up the section was a motor/generator and DC power was still applied to it, causing it to feed power back to the transformers. A relay in the controls should have fallen out when I pulled the oil switch but it failed.

Danger was part of the daily routine coal mining. If you were lucky, it was just a few stitches by a Chinese doctor. If you were unlucky, or just a little bit careless, the newspaper would be numbering the dependents you left behind.

Chapter 10 – Fire in the Hole

By now I was working in the Number 3 seam and was mechanically and electrically responsible for a complete section of machinery. Blasting coal required an explosive system known at the time as "Cardox," which was based on carbon dioxide and therefore safer in the mines than general explosives. Picture a piece of pipe about thirty inches long, with one end welded shut. The first eight or so inches from the front had holes bored at an angle toward the face of the coal seam. The other end had a screw-on head about six inches long, which contained an explosive. A thin strip of metal had been inserted between the screw-on head and the hollow remainder of the pipe.

A Cardox hole is drilled...

A dummy inserted...

Armed...

And detonated to blast the coal from the seam.

Wires were attached to the outward end of the screw-on part. The Cardox was carefully inserted into the hole drilled into the coal seam. "Dummies" were tamped into the hole. Dummies were about the size of a stick of dynamite and were homemade by the crew. They contained rock dust and the bags in which the rock dust came were cut up and used to make the dummies.

When all the Cardox were in place and wired—and the crew safely around the corner—a battery-powered plunger triggered the rupture of the thin strip of metal and the resulting explosion blew the coal outward and either onto the short pan line or onto the ground to be shoveled up. (Interestingly, the Cardox system is still widely used to clean silos and for rock excavation. It reportedly still uses the same factory in which it started in 1914.)

The coal company eventually abandoned rock dust and ordered ready-made dummies of clay. Once I was about three hundred feet down the main entry, bent over a job, when the crew put off a shot. A piece of clay hit me in the hind end. It felt like a bee sting.

The machine man and his helper were a team. One day the machine man had finished his cut and the driller had completed his drilling. The latter was ready to put the Cardox into the holes and was a couple short. His helper was already at the conveyor head and had trouble understanding just how many Cardox were needed. The machine man kept yelling "two-two." The helper kept yelling, "How many? How many?" Finally the machine man yelled loud as he could, "*T-U-E* you dumb SOB! "

When I had no breakdowns to work on I would sometimes help out by making such dummies. One day I was over in the air course splicing a cable and someone yelled, "Hey T.I., any dummies over there?"

"No, just me," I replied. I heard the man laughing as he crawled on up the entry.

The company decided to dispense with Cardox and consequently installed a compressed air system called Airdox. This system required a powerful air compressor with the ability to pipe air into the mines by way of a triple-strength pipe about an inch in diameter. Men were warned not to handle the pipe, as it was very

The Cardox explosive system was phased out in favor of a super-compressed air system, the Airdox.

dangerous if it ruptured. These pipes were installed on every section of the mine for blasting the coal cuts.

The Airdox system used a tubular instrument about eight feet long, which required a larger bit than the Cardox. On the end of the tube being inserted into the cut were holes which when activated blew compressed air out at a forty-five degree angle all around the end. On the back end was a hook-up for the copper tubing to deliver the air. Each entry was provided a blow down valve that ruptured the metal switch and thus triggered the force needed to blow the coal from the seam. The end where the copper pipe was attached also was had a thin strip of metal which was easily punctured by the air when released into the Airdox. The powerful air then burst outward to explode the coal from the seam.

On one shift two entries finished cutting coal at about the same time and each had one man insert the Airdox into the drilled hole. The copper tubing was long enough to allow the men to be around the corner when they opened the air valve. All explosions, whether Airdox, Cardox or dynamite, always were announced with a loud "Fire in the hole!"

On this shift it happened that a man in each room was inserting the Airdox into the hole at the same time. In one of the entries the man had only about half of his Airdox into the hole when the cry rang out. Both valves opened at the same time and both exploded.

The miner who had only half his Airdox in place was blown backward and it filled his face with blistering bits of coal and blew his hard top head off. He got no serious injuries but grabbed his hat with the light on it, stuck it under his arm and started running. Men in his crew saw him coming and one yelled, "There comes Red with his head under his arm!" I heard all this commotion and ran to the cut. I saw that Red was OK and everyone was still in good humor. However, we made arrangements so there would be no misunderstanding as to which crew member would open the valve.

Coincidentally, this compressed-air system was a great help to us repairmen, but not for the reason it was installed. We fashioned an air gun from some discarded tubing and used it to blow impacted coal dust from around any equipment we were working on.

One evening I was called upon to install a complete set of O-rings in a valve chest on a Joy loading machine. I went into the mine alone to do the job. It involved removing all the connecting hoses from all of the six or seven valves on the machine. Care had to be taken to identify each hose and coupling. This involved marking all the fittings and hoses going to each valve. My method of identifying them involved using electrical tape or a small wire or whatever I could find in order to track exactly where every hose came from.

After taking all the hoses loose and unbolting the valve set from the machine I prepared my work place. I was alone with no machinery running nearby. I listened intently to the methane gas coming from the coal seam and it sounded like a swarm of bees. Choosing a well-timbered location with a smooth bottom I rounded up a piece of relatively clean brattice cloth and, after taking a cap wedge and scraping the area clean, I spread the cloth out and laid the valve bank down, being careful to leave adequate space to the right and left.

I had brought a bag full of clean rags and proceeded to remove the two long bolts holding the individual valves together. I removed the bolts and began gently separating the valves, leaving a space of two inches or so between them. I opened the package containing the new set of O-rings. Taking a clean rag from my coveralls I wiped each valve down, removed the old O-ring and replaced them in each, being careful to remove any pieces of the old, ruptured rings. One by one I repeated the process until I had installed new rings in all the valves.

Now came the careful part. I had to assure that not a particle of coal dust or rock clung to the valves. I wiped the bolts clean and began re-assembling the machine. Inserting the bolts into the end of the valve assembly one by one I slid them into place until they were all separated slightly. I slowly began twisting the nuts on each bolt just a few threads at a time, one valve after another, until I had the assembly joined together again. After examining each valve and ensuring it fit tightly with no cracks I began the final tightening of the nuts.

By now it was time for lunch. After eating and resting I lifted the valve chest back onto the machine, reinstalled the bolts which attached them to the machine, and attached each hose in its proper place. I turned the machine on and allowed the oil to circulate a few times. I tried each valve in turn to assure there were no leaks. I tested each cycle of the machine's control to make sure it worked properly. A good morning's work.

Chapter 11 – Hitching a Ride on a Satellite

I paid attention to the technical improvements in mining machinery and I could read the handwriting on the wall and readied myself to grow with the machinery. As a new piece came in I made it my business to acquire a parts book and blueprints and would take them home for study. This allowed me to keep up with the advancements of new mining methods.

But with the responsibility of keeping the machinery running I knew something was lacking: I knew nothing of how electricity actually *worked.* I knew nothing of reading complicated blueprints or how to check out circuits visually or with instruments.

Too, I heard the steady drumbeat of The Future. I always read widely, including both science and science fiction, and knew that it wouldn't be long before man reached into outer space. I stood at the edge of a revolution in electronics, and a revolution in how we look at ourselves on this little planet.

State Street, Chicago, sometime in the 1950's. After living in the "holler" above Otsego, Chicago was overwhelming in its variety and color.

Either the United States or Russia would put a satellite in orbit soon, and then, who knows—might a human set foot on the moon? It was fantastic, literally, but it was coming true before my eyes.

The world I had grown up with seemed smaller by the day, as first radio and then television penetrated into the deep mountains little by little. I installed electrical power in both our house and my mother and father's house in Otsego and soon followed with telephone lines. I bought a Sears Silvertone radio and a year or two later bought our first television set, a large vacuum-tube console model. I ran a "channel four" antenna up the hillside above our house and we were able to see WOAY in Oak Hill. Not long after I bought an "all-channel" antenna and ran a line for it 1500 feet straight up the mountain. "All channels" turned out to be two more stations, but we didn't care; we were now part of the larger world.

Meanwhile I gradually eased into the life of a husband and father, in addition to trying to support my aged parents and sister Kathy who didn't marry until much later in life, all while fighting off the disturbing flashes of memory of what I had seen—and had done—during the war.

Little by little I introduced more foods into my diet, and my malaria attacks became less frequent. I gradually gained some of the normalcy I so desperately needed.

But I needed more; I needed to feel I was moving forward in this ever-smaller world. But ten years had elapsed since I was discharged from the service, so any GI Bill benefits I had coming to me had lapsed.

West Virginia has never been a particularly good launching pad for those with such ambitions and by now we had Gilbert, who came to us in 1946, and Gloria in 1950, but we were still in that little house until we were forced off the lease by the land company in 1956. We moved to the coal camp of Helen, in Raleigh County, as Recie was carrying our third child, David Thurman, born in 1957.

I decided to invest our meager savings to further advance my skills, so I enrolled in Coyne Electrical School in Chicago. I don't recall where I saw the ad for it but it must have been in the Beckley Post-Herald newspaper or on the back of Popular Mechanics or the like. Coyne's ads were spread widely, as they promised a large population of returning war vets an exciting career in radio and television repair, heating and air conditioning, and electrical repair.

Coyne was a big outfit, and those miners who, like me, were
thinking of the future were willing to invest the time and money
for their training.

VETERAN 26, desires job that will not
be affected in event of coal strike,
electrician 8 years experience, AC
and DC. high school graduate, graduate Coyne Electrical School, ICS
electrical operating engineering, also
5½ months U. S. Navy electrical
training schools. Write H. D. Parks,
Jr., Box 529, Sophia, W. Va., or see
me at my home in Midway.

I took the train from Prince, near Beckley, all the way to
Chicago. Coyne stood at 500 S. Paulina St and the school had
arranged a small place for me to stay on Jackson Boulevard, a few
blocks northwest of the school and about eight blocks west of the
famous Loop.

Chicago was and is an amazing city. I hated to be away from
my wife and children but I knew that our very existence as a
family—big family at that, with my parents ans sister and soon
three children—depended on my ability to provide.

This proved a wise move, for I was never without a job until I
retired in 1980. Coyne Electrical School provided me not
necessarily with a complete understanding of electricity but it gave
me the skills to teach myself as even newer technology came
along. How did Coyne compare with my earlier ambition to earn
money for one semester of college at a time? I'll never know, as I
never had the opportunity to attend college as such; I only know I
wanted to be something more than a general laborer.

The school was laid out in a series three-week courses, and I
purchased twelve weeks, or four sessions. They began with simple
fundamentals, wiring and repair, during which we learned the basic
rules of electricity as well as the construction, function, and
maintenance of small appliances and the vocabulary of
electricity—Ohm's law, amperes, voltage and how to use

combinations of all in order to come to a correct answer about why something worked, or didn't.

I had never been to Chicago. When I reported to the school the first thing I noticed was how diverse the school was, both in terms of the men there—they were almost all men—and the topics they intended to study.

By this time, the early 1950's, television was beginning to be very popular and the school had a program devoted primarily to this. Other courses dealt with

I don't recall Coyne reimbursing me for my travel to Chicago, but it was well worth my time and money. And I got to live in one of the great American cities.

manufacturing, motors large and small, wiring gauges for specific jobs, step-up and step-down transformers, and so on. I marveled at the evolution from mules to machinery and the revolution that remote control of machinery had wrought.

I soon returned to the mines but I had gotten my money's worth at Coyne and easily passed all my mining-related tests and certifications. I knew a lot more about the profession I had fallen

```
MS-950-B-1        WEST VIRGINIA DEPARTMENT OF EMPLOYMENT SECURITY        3  6  4  3
10/70             MANPOWER DEVELOPMENT AND TRAINING ACT
                  Referral Notice - Part-Time Training                  MDT CODE
Male [x]  Female [ ]                                 Project No.        (FP) 1036
Date of Birth:  11/26/20

   Miller, Thurman I.                    233-22-0166          Beckley EOC
          Name                              SSA No.              L. O.
   Box 205, Helen, W. Va.   25853
   Number    Street          City         State              ZIP Code
```

A. THIS SECTION TO BE COMPLETED BY SELECTION AND REFERRAL OFFICER

1. You have been selected to receive part-time training as a **Electrician Helper** under the provisions of Title II of the Manpower Development and Training Act of 1962, as amended.

| Number of weeks for which training is scheduled: 10 | Beginning Date: 4-19-71 |
| | Ending Date: 6-25-71 |

2. You may receive a part-time payment of $2 per session attended, not to exceed $10 a week. No payment will be made for training sessions that you fail to attend.

3. You should report to begin training: **Monday**   **April 19, 71**   **9:00**
   DAY   DATE   TIME
   at **Eastern Associated Coal Corp.**   **Herndon, W. Va. 24726**
   LOCATION OF TRAINING FACILITY
   Report to this individual **John Haley**

NOTE: If you find that you cannot report as directed, notify this office immediately.

Signature, Selection and Referral Officer   S. Andrews
Date   5-3-71

THIS SECTION TO BE COMPLETED BY TRAINEE

In consideration of my referral to training under the Manpower Development and Training Act as indicated above, I agree to report to the training facility as assigned, attend regularly, and do my best to master the training and to complete the course.

Signature of Trainee   Thurman I. Miller
Date   4/28/71

By the time I got my formal training certificate it was a formality—I had already been working on many, many pieces of high-voltage machinery for years. Nice to have it though.

into and was thereafter able to assess the trouble and get to the bottom of it much more quickly.

During the 1950's and 60's the mechanization of the coal industry accelerated. Just as when the old mules were literally put out to pasture, hand shovels rusted away and coal drills become obsolete, as did many of the hard-earned skills of the miners.

Many men were willing to learn the new machinery but were not necessarily tempered for it. One incident involved the first

Wilcox mine machines. One man had bid on the job to operate it. I had gone to work that morning to fix a breakdown on the machine and just finished when I saw a light coming at a fast crawl.

He rushed up to me. "T. I., I bid on the job of running this machine, can you teach me how to run it?"

The mine foreman had already started crawling up to see him.

"I'm only a mechanic, I don't do miracles," I said.

The companies dug more coal with fewer men and consequently accelerated the downsizing of their workforce. Thus began what many dubbed reverse migration, as men began traveling north to automobile factories or south to furniture mills, traveling the same roads their forefathers did in the last century but in the opposite direction—the "Hillbilly Highway."

Chapter 12 – Facing the Changes

I only heard my father curse once in my life. He was plowing the garden and the mare was a bit frisky and my father was having trouble plowing straight furrows. He finally picked up a rock and threw it at the mare, striking her hind end. "Calm down, you SOB!" It worked, and she did.

As I was growing up it eventually became my job to see that all the fires were built in winter time, so I had to be sure to have a full bucket of coal and an adequate supply of wood for the cook stove. One cold winter morning I got up and started to build the fire in the big pot-bellied stove in the living room. I had put a lot of mutton tallow on my boots and they were stiff, so I just kicked them off and one flew through the window with a tremendous crash. Dad heard the commotion and got out of bed. He took a look and told me to build the fire and then sit by the broken window. I nearly froze.

I have told elsewhere about how close I was with him, how I moved to the small coal camp of Helen because it was the only place I could find two houses close together for my family and for my mother, father, and sister Kathleen who stayed home to take care of them.

But on February 17th, 1965, my father died and I took the time off I was entitled to under our Union contract, to see to his burial.

My world was changing yet again. At Otsego I began to hear rumors that if things didn't pick up we would have to shut the mine down. But the mine at Otsego did pick up a good order and we resumed the five day week, with overtime occasionally. But I didn't think it could last. Not long after this I went to a mine at Tralee for several months. They had all Joy Manufacturing equipment—14BU loaders 6SC shuttle cars, and the Joy cutting machine. But when I went to Herndon they had different kinds of equipment. At first it was mostly Joy but later they brought in an entirely new assortment of Jeffrey machinery—shuttle cars, loaders, cutting machines. The electrical system employed by Jeffrey was different from Joy's. Their starting box had push connections as opposed to a threaded screw and clip ends with a hole for the screw. This equipment was continually breaking down due to mold collecting in their push connections.

Walter was a good chief to work for. The company hired a new section foreman, Milton Highchew, and after he had been there a couple of months he had run off every repairman Walter sent to his section. One morning Walter told me to bring my toolbox down to the section where this guy was foreman. I asked Walter what he had against me, that he would send me to this man's section. He just laughed and told me he wanted me to find out what the trouble was. "I know you will find a way to see," he said. The first day I went on his section he did not even speak to me except when something broke down.

After a few days he grunted at me and I just grunted back at him. Finally he broke down and began to talk to me. He said all the other guys were sorry excuses for repairmen and half the time he did not even know where they were. However, he said, as for me, every time I saw the crew busy shoveling coal I would be checking their machinery for potential breakdowns. After a few months he told me he at first thought I was crazy for checking equipment that he knew was running properly. He was friendly with me from then on.

Walter told me later that if anybody could figure Milton out it would be me.

By now the Number 3 seam at Otsego was about to play out. They had already mined the Beckley seam on the mountaintop, where I started, and worked their way down to Number 3 and 4. Two or three days of work a week were the norm. The Super kept saying we would try it for another month or so and if things did not improve the mine would close down. This began to play on my nerves so I decided to apply for employment elsewhere.

My neighbor told me they were hiring at the Herndon mine, just south of Mullens, at a mine owned by the Koppers Coal Company, so I went there and asked Superintendent Jim Murphy for a job. He merely told me I was hired and to go get signed up. I proceeded to explain I had no experience with DC power and that all I could promise was a fair day's work, and that I would make mistakes but would not be afraid to admit them. He replied, "Just go get signed up and come out on the third shift. Don't come and ask me to get off it, because that's what I'm hiring you for."

I planned to report to the new job on March 1. I was still working at Otsego and before going up to the new mine I went into the office and told the Superintendent at Otsego I was leaving. He kept trying to talk me out of leaving until I almost missed the man trip for my shift. I had worked at Otsego nineteen years and he and I both knew, almost by instinct, that if one of his older miners left others would soon follow suit, and that's what happened.

Herndon was a big mine—I learned later that you could travel underground in that mine all the way underground directly between the towns of Keystone and Welch, a distance of more than seven miles.

At Herndon some of the coal seam was very low, some average, about 42 inches high, and a few places somewhat higher. At Herndon I was the first man hired as electrician/mechanic on the hoot owl shift and having been there the longest I was soon designated shift leader.

While I was working at Herndon the powers that be came up with the idea of a certification process for us electricians. studied hard for it. (I took the material home and Recie and I were sitting out in our swing. I had her asking the exam questions and when she came to the word "diode" she called it a *di-o-dee*. I started laughing so hard I almost fell out of the glider. She got up, slammed the book down the said, "That's the last time I'll help you." The grin on her face may have been a snarl.)

The first exam they created was long, many paragraphs of eight or ten lines each. We had to carefully study each of these and then answer each in almost exactly the same words as the question was phrased. The exam took almost eight hours. I passed the exam with flying colors.

This new certification process later caused trouble, however. They passed a law which forbade an electrician to take the bolts out of a starting box unless he had passed the exam. A veteran electrician who could not pass the exam was prohibited from opening the box and had to find one of the new men to do it. But when the new kid got the box uncovered he didn't know what to do with it. Thus, some of the older miners who failed the test found themselves unqualified even to remove the top from the starter boxes on the high voltage machinery.

Later, after realizing this sort of test—parroting answers from the preparation materials—was not an accurate gauge of a man's ability, they switched to multiple-choice questions, which made it easier to pass. They had a lot of younger people take the test and those who passed were on a probationary status and were required to wear a red helmet. They were immediately qualified to open the starters—but after they did so they still often had to track down one of the "unqualified" older miners to show them what to do inside it.

AV versus DC

DIRECT CURRENT (DC)

ALTERNATING CURRENT (AC)

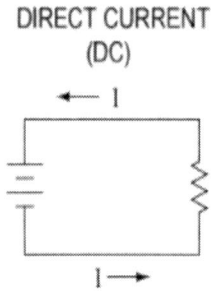

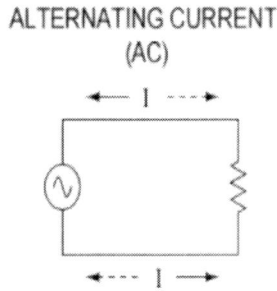

DC is the kind of electricity made by a battery (with definite positive and negative terminals), or the kind of charge generated by rubbing certain types of materials against each other. As useful and as easy to understand as DC is, it is not the only "kind" of electricity in use. Certain sources of electricity naturally produce voltages alternating in polarity, reversing positive and negative over time. Either as a voltage switching polarity or as a current switching direction back and forth, this "kind" of electricity is known as Alternating Current of AC. Whereas the familiar battery symbol is used as a generic symbol for any DC voltage source, the circle with the wavy line inside is the generic symbol for any AC voltage source. Why would anyone bother with AC. In some cases AC holds no practical advantage over DC. In applications where electricity is used to dissipate energy in the form of heat, the polarity or direction of current is irrelevant, so long as there is enough voltage and current to the load to produce the desired heat (power dissipation). However, with AC it is possible to build electric generators, motors and power. Alternating current distribution systems that are far more efficient than DC, and so we find AC used predominantly across the world in high power applications.

For about six months it was the only electrician on the hoot owl shift and many times I would spend the whole shift alone, which I did not like but stuck it out anyhow. The work here was not unlike what I had been used to except it was DC power instead of AC. Having attended Coyne, though, I soon adapted. (Both types of current can kill you equally, but are used for different power needs and thus the equipment form factor and voltage calculations are different for the two.)

The drift mouth was a slope about three hundred feet on a steep angle but had a belt line which we could ride. Up the entry was a charging station for a little three-wheel buggy. This is where I kept my toolbox and most of the time when I had a repair job to do I could just load my toolbox on the buggy and wheel myself right up to the machine I was to work on.

Early in my time at Herndon I noticed they used a different method of roof support. At Otsego they had used timbers and I had grown accustomed to gauging the condition of the roof by the sound of the timbers as they first groaned and then began to crack, as they took on the weight of the mountain. If timbers began to break it was time set additional timbers.

At Herndon they used roof bolts, which I at first distrusted. Roof bolts are shot up directly into the roof layers and act to keep the several layers intact. Scientifically, they're more reliable than shoring up a roof from below after it's begun to disintegrate.

Later I learned to respect the bolting system and saw it worked even better than timbers. But when I first I looked down a long section with not a timber in sight I naturally felt afraid; but I went on to the job I had to do.

Generic	Schottky	Shockley	Constant current

Zener	Light-emitting	Photo-	Step recovery

Tunnel	Varactor	PIN	Vacuum tube

A = Anode
K = Cathode

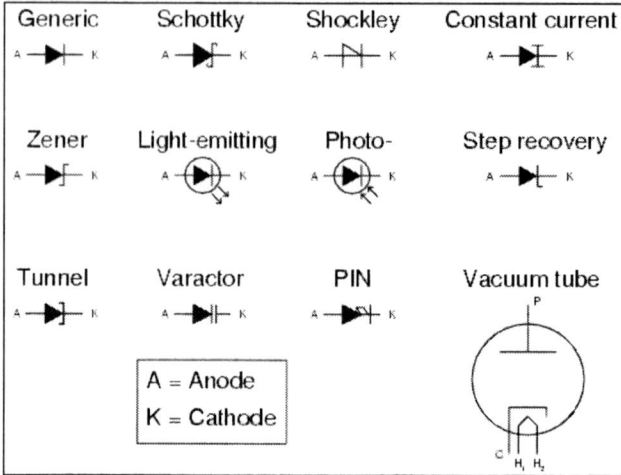

The many types of diodes, from Lessons In Electric Circuits, Tony R. Kuphaldt. Used under the Design Science License.

At Herndon I discarded much of what I'd learned at Otsego and put in even more time studying at home. One night the evening shift was in the process of moving the equipment for a section to another location. The cutting machine was DC-powered. The shift foreman told me the machine quit running just when their quitting time came and they left it for us to cope with. I knew the machine had a diode—which allows current to travel in only one direction—so I told the man who was going to run the machine to check where they had plugged it in. He did and I asked had they changed the power connectors He said they had the positive on the ground wire. I yelled for him to change them back. The machine then worked properly.

Since I was the senior man on the repair crew, when they hired a new electrician they always had me work with him a month or so to show him the ropes. Once they hired a man who evidently thought he was too good for the job. He never got himself dirty and never took off his gloves, even though some jobs a man could not do with gloves on. One night we were installing a tree of leads in a loader and he was trying his best not to get dirty.

I crawled round to his side and told him in no uncertain words to take off his gloves, get his screwdriver out and start digging. He took one look at my face and did exactly what I told him to do. I did not keep him on my shift very long.

As the company began hiring new men a couple started on the same day that we just happened to be working in the worst section in the mine. They were not mechanics, just general labor, and took one look at the bad top and broken timbers and said, "Hell fire, this is worse than where we used to work." They piled onto the belt and left.

But I came to learn that electricians are always on call. No power meant no work; no work, no coal; no coal, no profit.

One night I was working at Herndon and the power suddenly went out. All the phones began to ring and everyone wanted to know what happened. My answer to each was the same, "I do not know. When I know, you will know." I started walking toward the belt head. When I got there I noticed a rock-dusting machine sitting in the walk way. Looking across the belt I noticed a cap wedge nailed to a cable.

On close examination I found the wedge had been nailed into the high voltage cable, shorting it out. The two men handling the rock duster had made the mistake. It was a miracle no one was killed. Their confusion stemmed from the fact that the high voltage cable and the DC cable were the same size, so it was an honest mistake.

After making sure all disconnects and oil switches were pulled I set about splitting the insulation and taping up the hole which had grounded the high voltage. I restarted the power and later returned to make a permanent splice according to federal regulations.

The company got in a section of AC equipment and, knowing I had 19 years' experience with this type power, they gave me the section to maintain. When something on this section broke down it was my place to investigate and take care of the problem. One night I went alone on the section to repair the loader. When I got off the belt I looked on up the entry toward the machine and noted a blue haze hovering a couple feet below the top. I did not know what it was but began to investigate.

The company had failed to secure the air-delivering canvas barriers and the machine was overheating, especially with the dampness beneath, making a fog just above it. That indicated that no fresh air was getting to it.

I used a good bit of my time on that shift correcting the mistake, putting up canvas to the working face to direct fresh circulating air to it. I knew methane was colorless and you could not smell it, and only a methane tester could find it, and you didn't take any chances with it.

But there was always pressure from the mine operators—many of whom came into the mines rarely if at all—to cut corners to produce more coal.[4] I understood that; the coal industry is cutthroat-competitive, but I did not want to be a statistic. Luckily, I had the union behind me and could refuse to work in a place I deemed unsafe.

Mr. Murphy, the Superintendent, was a good man but very strict and hands-on in maintaining his equipment. When I first got to Herndon the mine still operated as The Premier Coal Company. Eastern Associated Coal Corporation had bought it but it still operated under the Premier name. It was made plain that he had to approve anything related to repair work. For example, the second shift reported a burst hydraulic hose on a loader not far into the mine. He left word for me to go inside, remove the hose, and bring it to his house so he could see that it was really a bad hose. They had no supply man at that time so he gave me the key to the supply house and told me to get the replacement hose and record it on the books.

Later on, after Eastern took over, they hired a full-time supply man. They gave him a list of names that could get supplies. One night the second shift left a transmission off a loader torn down and had already called out for several bearings, which we took inside with us. Down in the bottom of the transmission was a small bearing they had missed. It turned out to be the only thing really bad on the transmission.

I got the bearing out and took it outside and up to the supply house. The supply man looked at the bearing, then looked at me and asked my name. I told him and he informed me I could not have the new bearing because my name was not on the list. We traded a few choice words, to no avail, and I turned to leave.

"One more thing," I said, "I got a loader down and in the morning about seven o'clock I am calling my boss to tell him why it's still down. Meanwhile you better have a good answer for *your* boss."

---

[4] See the discussion of the Upper Big Branch explosion below, for example.

I got almost to the door and he yelled, "Hey, wait a minute." He brought me the bearing. Later he learned I had been in the Marine Corps, as he had been. We become pretty good friends.

My work at Herndon was similar to that at Tralee and Otsego as far as maintenance was concerned—fixing broken cables and chains, preventive maintenance, and so on. In addition to repairing breakdowns reported by the evening shift it was routine to spend extra minutes or hours, in some cases, testing starting boxes with a feeling gauge to see if they were permissible.

By this time the company had hired a few more electrician/mechanics. Since I was the oldest in years and time with the company they declared me shift leader. When I would report to work the

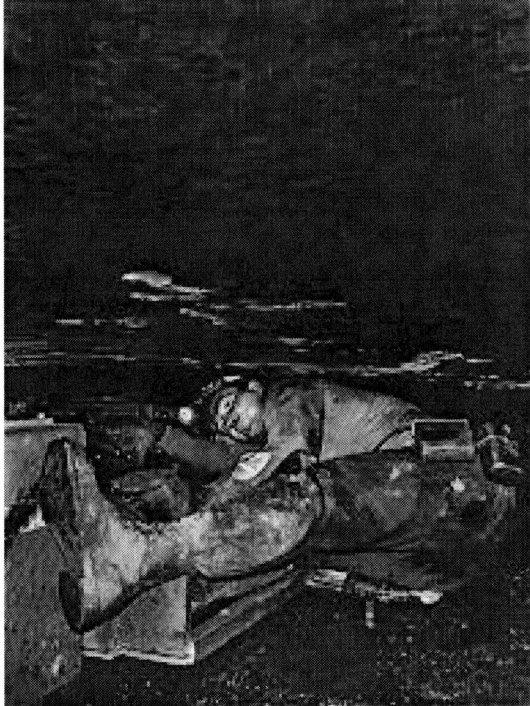

A typical position for fixing mine machinery, sometimes for two straight shifts.

second shift section foremen handed me their work schedule, their list of breakdowns. I would look over their report and dispense the jobs to the rest of the electricians, always keeping in mind which man would be best for a specific job. Mostly, at first, the few new men respected me for my age, experience and position as shift leader.

Before long the company decided to invest in a section of AC equipment. Consequently they got in the complete assortment of power units such as breaker boxes, load centers, and the long cables necessary to run the equipment. They had brought in a load center, a big box about 40' long, 42" wide and 42" high, which connected three or more high-voltage transformers.

All three transformers needed for AC power had female connections to the outside, both the primary and secondary circuits, and for reasons unknown to me it had been left in a breakthrough next to the belt line. They left me orders to move it on over into the air course so they could hook something to it and pull it up onto the section.

After I collected the breakdown reports and had designated them to the other repair men I failed to give one man anything. "What about me?" he asked.

"Oh, I want you to help me move that load center over to the air course."

Then he asked if the other men were going to help. Shucks, I said, it's just one load center. He just looked at me. Meanwhile, I had already told the supply boss what I needed—four long belt rollers, four eight-foot header boards, and a lifting jack. The rest of the men left and he and I crawled onto the belt. We got off by the load center. I had him take the jack to the end next to the air course and jack up the loader center about twelve inches. Then we placed the long headers, one on each side of the load center, and punched the belt rollers as far under it as we could. Then I told him to let it down. After removing the jack I told him to go start pushing. He did and the load center started rolling along. I heard him say "Well, I'll be damned." In a few minutes the load center was where they told me to leave it. Some jobs are just common sense.

When they got the load center, the Joy loader, cutting machine, shuttle cars and the rest of the equipment, the hoot owl boss asked me to take care of hooking everything up. The load center came with a five hundred-foot long cable with a large coupling on each end. When the supply gang brought in the cable I looked at the coupling and told them they had put the wrong end first and we had to change ends with it.

One said, "All we can do is unload it, so all of us started dragging one end of it down the walk way."

"Just a minute guys, I got a better idea," I said.

I put one man on the remote button and told him to keep his eye on the belt so it could be stopped if necessary. I loaded the end of the cable and put two of the men to feeding the rest of the cable onto the belt and let the belt do all the work. When they came to the other end all they had to do was start the belt backing up to where the load center was. Problem solved with a minimum of manual labor.

The chief told me I was to take care of any breakdowns in this AC section, in addition to still acting as shift leader. But every time one of the other repairmen had something they couldn't handle they got on the phone and started calling me and kept it up till I answered. One night I sent the same man who had helped me with the loader and his buddy on a job where the continuous miner was and when I got there I asked what the trouble was.

They told me they could not get a big three-inch nut off the shaft. I applied a trick I had learned. I took my ballpeen hammer off my belt, got an ax, and put the round peen of the hammer on the nut and hit it a few times, then placed the hammer on another part of the nut till I had gone all around it several times. Then I placed the sharp blade of the ax on the nut and pecked on it gently until I made a gash on the nut. Then I started hitting the ax with my hammer. It started moving and in just a minute I pitched the nut over on their side, where they were resting. "Here's your nut." (I almost said, "You're nuts.")

This AC section was not unlike all the sections of a mine— slate falls occurred at unexpected times and places. Once, a loading machine was being trammed out of a break when a huge slab of rock came bursting down and broke in two, leaving half of it on top of the loader and another huge piece lying at an angle down by the control box. The opposite side containing the reset and tramming valves was undamaged. The machine would not start, which forced me to crawl on my belly up to the lid which contained all the contacts. Something had jarred loose inside it. I managed to turn on my side in order to get my tools out of my pouch.

After an agonizing half hour lying on my side I managed to get all the bolts out of the lid. I found and corrected the trouble and backed out of the hole and went around and lifted the reset. The machine came on and I went back under the rock and finally replaced the lid. I didn't take time to ensure an air-tight lid, though I knew I would have to do that after they got the rock off and the machine moved. They brought the cutter around and attached a cable to the loader and the operator of the loader tried to tram at the same time the cutter started backing up.

But the loader never moved and finally they borrowed a couple of railroad jacks and managed to lift the huge rock enough to get it free.

The danger of fire in a mine is omnipresent. Even the Exhibition Coal Mine in Beckley has a fire boss. If a fireboss goes into a mine and finds something wrong he would take a half-header, about twenty-four by 18 by two inches, and write *Danger* on it in chalk. If no foreman was there, us working men moved to another section. They had hired another foreman who then was in charge of everyone who worked the third shift in the Barkers' Creek mine. He crossed out *Danger* and wrote *OK* and asked for a volunteer to ride back and check it out. All refused, under the threat of being fired for crossing the danger board. Finally he said, "You guys got four hundred men backing you up and I got nobody but me." He rode back and cleared whatever the problem was.

A new foreman of the third shift came to me one night and asked me if I would consider being a troubleshooter. Other electricians by now had become somewhat used to the AC section so I told him that was OK by me. He just told me to pick out a spot where he could reach me by phone. I liked this job for awhile but I was still considered as shift leader.

But some of the men objected to my being a shift leader, as most of them knew me as just a working guy like them. They wanted a real boss. There was a meeting with the brass and when the meeting opened none of the men spoke up.

Finally I explained the problem to the Super, mine foreman and shift foremen, and then I left. I reported at my usual time that night but told the shift foremen that tomorrow night I would be getting there just in time for shift change and he or someone else could take breakdown reports and assign whomever he wanted to the job. I told him I would no longer be shift leader but just a plain maintenance man like the rest. He told me he knew nothing of how to dispense the repairmen, so I advised him on how to do that.

Not my problem. From then on I arrived at the belt just before my shift would start.

Chapter 13 - Resurfacing

My work, despite the challenge of constantly learning about very high-voltage equipment, began to seem somewhat routine. A job here, a job there, too many to remember in detail. An opening became available in the mine shop, above ground, repairing locomotives. My being the most senior of the qualified men, it was mine if I wanted it. I did. I had done my time underground.

Giles Holt had been in the shop for quite some time and knew a lot more about locomotives than I did. He was about the same age as my son Gilbert. He was a quiet man and was very patient with me while I learned the ropes. I quickly learned the process of preventive maintenance on these machines. We worked mostly on two types of locomotives, a smaller one of fifteen tons and a larger one of forty tons.

The small one was powered by what we called a set of trucks.

A more modern man-trip, covered for the miner's protection.

A unit consisted of four locomotive wheels just like you see on a railroad car, only a bit smaller. Between the wheel axles was a hundred-horsepower motor and the big gearbox had a metal box around it, which we had to make sure had the proper amount of oil in it. The four wheels also had brake shoes, exactly like those in a big railroad car. These wore out quickly depending on working conditions in the mine and the habits of the operator. If his motor encountered a damp, slick rail and the wheels started to spin the operator would put sand on the rails, and we also had to take care of these sandboxes.

The forty-ton locomotive had two sets of trucks. When a motor went down in one of these it was necessary to literally lift one end of the forty-ton locomotive up high enough to push the trucks out from under the machine. This was accomplished with a huge overhead hoist which was designed to travel forward, backward, and side to side. After lifting the machine and rolling the trucks out from under the machine they were trammed to the other end of the shop and let down on the floor.

After the hundred-horsepower motor was replaced and all other components examined and repaired as needed the process was reversed, the hoist again attached, the trucks moved into place, and the locomotive lifted up. The trucks were adjusted as needed for the machine to be let down on them again. Then all the parts were reinstalled and checked. This process usually involved most of an entire shift to complete, assuming of course that nothing else was found wrong with the locomotive.

We replaced the motor on the fifteen-ton locomotive the same way, though obviously with less effort. As time went on I thought to myself, "There has to be a better way." I discussed my idea with my buddy Giles and told him exactly what I had in mind. He thought about it for awhile and said it had never been tried before but he agreed it could work. My idea was that instead of lifting the locomotive up we use the hoist to set the new motor down in the pit. We unhooked everything attached to the bad motor.

The motors had a large nut, about one inch, welded to the top of the motor. We made up an eye hook and screwed it to the old motor and unhooked the remaining parts, holding it up, and just let the old motor down into the pit. Then using the hoist we trammed the locomotive down over the new motor in the pit, replaced the eye hook, and proceeded to lift the new motor back up in place, leaving the hoist attached until we replaced the remaining components. Then we removed the hook and proceeded with the repair. We completed this whole process in about half the time as compared to the other way.

This process also required that a big four-inch nut be loosened and removed, which was sometimes difficult. Again I thought about it a while. There was no socket that size in existence. When we finally got the one nut loose and off I took it over to my tool cabinet. I found a piece of hard cardboard paper, laid the nut down on it, and traced its outline. I found some scraps of three-eighth by two-inch pieces of flatiron. I measured the six points of the outline and cut pieces out, and using the big grinding wheel fashioned six pieces while laying the pieces on the drawing. When I had all six made to fit my drawing I started welding them together. Giles asked what I was building. "A big socket," I told him.

I cut six short pieces of one inch by three-eighths inches. I welded one on each side of the socket at a forty-five degree angle and welded all of them pretty heavily. Then I used the cutting torch to cut off the protruding parts and the grinding wheel to smooth it all out. I found a piece of one-inch round iron and cut a hole through the six pieces and welded the iron in the center of it.

Finally I welded a big ring on the other end of the rod. Next time we had a motor to change the big socket fit exactly. We used a four-foot rod for leverage and off came the nut with no fuss. These locomotives operated on five hundred volts on the main contacts. The control circuit operated from a bank of six batteries hooked up to a much smaller voltage. We had to check them every shift to make sure they had adequate water.

The locomotives were also equipped with an air compressor. Each contact had a small air valve which was operated by the low-voltage battery circuit. When the operator turned on the controller to move the motor the low voltage was automatically applied to the air valve, and the compressed air made the power contact come on to make contact to the high voltage. The control circuit and headlight circuit all operated from the battery pack and were on the opposite end from the operator.

Just imagine the several control wires traveling front to back on a forty-foot locomotive. This was somewhat difficult to troubleshoot when there was trouble.

We used a voltmeter but power remained on the locomotive and it was dangerous. Again I thought, "Gotta be a safer way." The inside of the mine had a series of battery-operated phones and when they began to weaken their batteries were changed out but still had a lot of power left, just as any consumer battery might retain. As I came through town I stopped and bought a simple doorbell ringer. I took one of these discarded batteries and made a circuit tester out of it. Now we could troubleshoot a circuit without main power being on the machine. (When I had to retire one of the men who took my place asked me if I would let him keep the tester, which I did.)

In addition to the locomotives we also had to service portal buses and jeeps. This involved a lot of sitting down on the hard floor. With my cap light on I had to tilt my head way down in order to see what I was looking for. "Gotta be a better way," I thought again. The next night I found some eighth-inch flatiron and proceeded to make an adaptation so that when I placed it where my cap light went it tilted my hat down on a forty five degree angle. That way my light shone where I was walking and also just where I was looking on the control panel.

One night they brought in a portal bus—a self-propelled transport car for eight to twelve men—and said it wouldn't shut off; every time they put the trolley pole on it started off by itself. I got inside, set the brakes firmly, went back to the control panel, sat down and turned off my light. When my buddy came by I told him to put power on the bus when I yelled. I watched the panel closely when power was applied.

The wheels started spinning and I saw a little streak of fire crawling along in the panel. I yelled to take the power off and turned my light back on and began to examine where I saw the fire. Carbon had built up between two terminals and shorted out the circuit. I got my knife and screw driver and cleaned all the carbon off down to where I could see paint on the board. I powered on the bus.

Nothing happened so I left the power on, released the brakes and trammed the bus forward and back and everything worked as it should.

One night we were busy working on a locomotive when all of a sudden we heard the sound of a lot of gunfire coming from the direction of the town, which was only a few hundred yards away. We heard the ping of bullets hitting the shop. We found out later that two gangs were trying to break into a store and were not aware of each other until they exchanged gunfire. A police patrol car happened along, the officer adding his gun to the firefight. Not knowing exactly what was happening we beat a hasty retreat down into the pit and waited until the gunfire ceased.

Another time during August a severe storm came roaring through the country. Being a hot night we had the huge doors open at both ends of the shop. We paid little attention to it until the wind got stronger and we began to see paper plates, paper cups, leaves and pieces of tree limbs going straight through the shop. Using the remote we slid the pit cover almost shut, leaving just enough room to retreat down into the pit.

Herndon Robbery Is Being Probed

MULLENS (RNS) — State and county police are investigating the forced entry of the Blankenship Service Station at Herndon during Friday night.

Deputy Sheriff Vernie Morgan said the station management reported the theft of several cartons of cigarets, candy, and between $20 and $30 cash.

Entrance to the building was gained through a rest room window.

One morning the shop boss came in and started quarreling about so much junk laying around in the shop, seeming to blame me and Giles. I said, "Well, it's hard for us to determine the difference between equipment and junk, so get a red chalk and a white chalk and mark all you think is junk with a red mark and what's good with white chalk." Sure enough, the next night several things bore a red mark and we dutifully loaded them up and rolled them outside.

Next morning he came through the door and looked around until he spied us and started complaining about rolling stock on the floor, grease spots, several other things. This kept up for about a week until I got fed up with it. I told Giles that when the boss came that night just to follow my lead. As the boss came in I told Giles, let's go.

We started toward the boss, pointing a finger at him and bitching about how the other shift left oil and scraps of metal on the floor—just anything else we could think of. Next morning we did the same thing. We didn't give him a chance to spot us; we spotted him and repeated what we had done the day before.

The next morning when he came through the door he saw us first and instead of coming toward us he made a hasty retreat to the office. Then one morning he sought us out. "I want to tell you boys something but just keep it under your hat. I made a mistake and turned in an extra shift for you both that you didn't work. So just keep a record of your overtime and just pay me back like that."

We made it our business to start work early and if we had a motor to work on we worked some in the morning. In about a week we told him we were square. "So soon?" he asked. We showed him where we had the equivalent overtime, money wise, to amount to a shift.

There are ways to get bosses off your back.

One night they brought all the jeeps in for a complete check because mine inspectors were coming. Next morning the chief electrician came through and asked if all the fire extinguishers worked. I told him yes, and he asked "How the h——l do you know?" "I tried them all," I replied. He just stared at me. After he left Giles laughed and told me I shouldn't talk to the chief like that. I told him the chief ought not to ask such a stupid question. That same day the chief came bursting through the door about five minutes after the motor man had pulled in a locomotive. "T.I, what's wrong with that motor?"

A motorman at work.

"It's broken down."

"I know it's broke down; I want to know what the trouble is."

"Don't know yet, can't see down through the covers."

Giles just looked at me with a smile on his face. We took the covers off and located the trouble but by now it was quitting time and we left it for the day shift, after pointing out the trouble to them, of course.

One night Giles failed to show up for work. It was winter and about ten below. I started whatever work was in there and about one-thirty in the morning the furnace quit. It didn't take long for the cold to invade the shop. I went out to the big oil tank, climbed up and unscrewed the nut, and took out the long stick used to check the oil level. I let it hit bottom, pulled it out. Dry. Someone had failed to order oil.

I knew right away I was not going to work all night without heat so I found a DC bonder. (This is the same as a welder running on alternating current, but runs on DC.) I got some canvas and built a leanto against the wall. The only time I left it was when the phone rang. The chief came walking in about six-thirty and asked why in the blank it was so cold. I unhooked the bonder, picked up my dinner bucket, and on the way out I told him the shop was out

109

of oil. I heard him cursing as I went out the door.

One night I found a three-eighths drill in the trash bin. All the handles had been broken off. I added a wire and plug to it and plugged it in and it ran fine. The next night I saw it had been thrown away again. I found it in the trash again and took it out and put it in my car, brought it home and constructed myself a bench drill with a handle to pull down. I also attached a mercury tube so when I pulled it down it automatically came on and when the spring-loaded handle was released it pulled up and shut itself off.

Recycling was and remains part of my being. Use it, don't abuse it; if it breaks, fix it.

Chapter 14 – United We Stood

Working conditions in the early days of mining were deplorable, leading to short, brutal lives for the miners and in many cases poverty for their families. The rise of the United Mine Workers and other unions in the early part of the 20th century union led to many battles between the union and mining companies. Many of the most notable conflicts were in West

The great John L. Lewis, president of the UMWA and a hero to many miners. A maker of kings in the political world during the days of coal's dominance.

Virginia, such as the so-called Battle of Blair Mountain, the largest armed uprising since the Civil War; the 1920 shootout between miners and Baldwin-Felts detectives that became known as the Matewan Massacre; and the retributive assassination of Sid Hatfield and Ed Chambers on the steps of the McDowell County courthouse two years later. Coal extraction seems fueled by blood. The violence went on and on, as the miners fought to form a union strong enough to take on the immensely wealthy and politically connected coal barons.

For a variety of reasons, during the Depression and war years the union became more powerful and its influence spread widely under the leadership of John L. Lewis.

For many years it was a strong political power in the coal fields. And, truth be told, the union saved a lot of miners' lives, and made their post-working years survivable, by bargaining for stricter safety rules, more robust monitoring for methane and other dangers, and negotiating decent pension and health insurance benefits.

The union was a central part of miners' lives, and of our families' lives. My wife Recie's father, Dewey Marshall, was a union official, the president of Union local 6195, and my son Gilbert married the daughter of Dennis Saunders, president of the UMWA's District 29. Did the union overreach in later years, with more frequent and possibly unnecessary strikes, with demands that cut into the reasonable need for a company to earn a profit? Probably.

But as I was forming myself into a miner the union was sometimes all that stood between the companies and naked profit extracted at the cost of working men's lives.

Even when I was serving my country in the Marine Corps coal was never far away.

When I came to mining our nation had just won a world war during which the U. S. government detained a coal miner just as they drafted a man into the military service of his country; if they were of age they were detained or deferred from the draft if needed to mine coal, which powered our nation's factories. During this time of turmoil the union still retained its power and each mine functioned under the rules laid down by the union, in cooperation with the coal companies. Labor was king.

When I first went to work in the industry in 1945 I found out it was not a question of *whether* you wanted to join the union, but more of a statement that if you wish to work in this mine, you *will* join.

At that time, each man who went to work appeared in a union meeting and was asked to take an oath. Part of the oath was: "Do you swear not to reveal the names of any union member to the company?" I knew the union was powerful at that time and this seemed a strange holdover from its earliest days, when joining a union could get a man killed.

Local UMWA chapters were operated by committee, with a president, vice president, and safety committee composed of three members of the union. A secretary, treasurer and financial secretary rounded out

Before the rise of the UMWA, the poitical deck was definitely stacked against the miner and in favor of the coal operator.

the leadership. A mine committee made up of three members handled grievances with the company. If a member felt he was mistreated by the company over what job he was to do he took his case to the committee which in turn took it up with the company, and more often than not an agreement was reached. Sometimes the company balked and refused to give in and a strike would follow. Sometimes miners would strike without the permission of union leadership, referred to as a "wildcat" strike.

When an individual brought his case before the mine committee he was asked to explain in detail what his grievance was. He was then

113

asked three questions: "Did you violate a company rule, state law or federal regulation?"

After finding out exactly what this individual had done (or didn't do—sometimes the issue was a miner refusing to work in what he considered unsafe conditions) the mine committee determined whether he had a legitimate grievance. The committee's decision was then voted on and the case resolved one way or the other with the company.

This shows the power the union once wielded. Even from the first, but accelerating after mid-century, companies began to find the numerous loopholes in their contracts with the union, such as closing down a unionized mine and reopening it later under the name of another company not a signatory to the union contract.

ADDRESS
OF THE
PRESIDENT
TO THE
COAL MINERS
MAY 2, 1943, AT 10.00 P.M.,E.W.T.
NATIONALLY BROADCAST

My Fellow Americans:

I am speaking tonight to the American people, and in particular to those of our citizens who are coal miners.

Tonight this country faces a serious crisis. We are engaged in a war on the successful outcome of which will depend the whole future of our country.

This war has reached a new critical phase. After the years that we have spent in preparation, we have moved into active and continuing battle with our enemies. We are pouring into the world-wide conflict everything that we have -- our young men, and the vast resources of our nation.

I have just returned from a two weeks' tour of inspection on which I saw our men being trained and our war materials made. My trip took me through twenty States. I saw thousands of workers on the production line, making airplanes, and guns and ammunition.

Everywhere I found great eagerness to get on with the war. Men and women are working long hours at difficult jobs and living under difficult conditions without complaint.

Along thousands of miles of track I saw countless acres of newly ploughed fields. The farmers of this country

President Roosevelt used his May 2, 1943, Fireside Chat to respond to a coal strike by the UMWA by using federal troops to take over the mine. Coal was essential to the war effort.

When the union entered a new contract not long after I started working it established a system where jobs were awarded on the basis of seniority rather than at the whim of management. I was elected and served for several years as recording secretary of UMWA Local 6195. One of the pledges when joining the union was that a member would not reveal the name of another member, lest the company blackball active union members. Thus, only two men connected with the company would have access to the union member list, the superintendent and the recording secretary, so I was privy to its content a week before it was presented to the local union for approval. By this time the company had opened a mine on the opposite mountain, Number 4 . Number 3 was still being mined and miners from both mines were included on the list.

I have included on the DVD version of this book the audio of FDR's 1943 Fireside Chat in which he directs coal miners back to work, or else federal troops would see that they returned. But, how can Uncle Sam make a man put in a day of work?

As Number 3 was beginning the process of closing some of the younger men were transferred to Number 4 since Number 3 was working only about three days per week. An argument ensued in the local union as to whether the seniority list should be split into two separate lists, one for Number 4 and one for Number

Three. It was to be put to a vote.

I stood up in the meeting and asked the president for the floor. To the local union I said, "I want you men of Number 4 to consider the consequences before your final vote. As you know, the remaining men in Number 3 are the older workers who would have trouble passing a doctor's exam, which the company had previously stated would be required. You are sticking a knife in their backs before they are eligible for retirement. So please let the one seniority list stand and do not divide our membership."

Nevertheless, they voted to have two separate lists.
In my nineteen years at Otsego I filled three separate union offices, Secretary, Financial Secretary and Treasurer. The district put out a memo dictating that an auditing committee be elected to audit the books. Well and good, I said. They elected two men to audit the books and sent the books to the district office. The district returned them and rejected the audit. The same men audited them a second time but it was again returned as inadequate to function as an audit. The president of the local asked me what we should do about it. "Pay me the money you were paying them and I will audit them myself." So they agreed and I presented the district with my own audit. The return memo to the secretary read simply "approved." Problem solved. In a year or so I was elected treasurer and served for several years in that office.

There was a radical element in the union in those days—as there always is in every union. When election time came they outnumbered the sober-minded members and put their own men in charge. The man elected in my place asked when he could pick up the books. After I brought them up to date I notified him a few days later and came up one Saturday morning and I turned them over to him. He had no idea what he was getting into. A week later he brought the books back to me and asked me to take back the job. I typed out a statement to this effect and told him to have every other officer in the local to sign off on it, which he did. He told me later he did not want the damned job to start with.

My final office was financial secretary. Every time someone retired I had to approve his papers and put the local's seal on them. One day a huge black man brought some blank papers and told me to seal them and he would fill them out later. I handed them back to him. "Sorry, get them properly filled and bring them back." As he left I heard some profanity.

Another man who lived in Caloric had run his wife off and gotten another woman in her place. He came up to the house and asked me to have her put on his hospital card—the union had excellent medical benefits. Fine, I said, bring your marriage certificate and I will take care of it. "Oh, we ain't married," he replied. Again I explained the rules and he turned and left.

The UMWA is not the industrial powerhouse it once was, has been in decline for along time for a variety of reasons, not least the increased productivity and decline in mine employment of the 1950's, and the deep corruption that took hold of the UMWA in the 1960's.[5]

I think of the union's rise and fall from power as something akin to the rise and fall of the Roman Empire—but the union, at least in theory, remains an important counterweight to the powerful coal companies.

In reading the Union's account of what happened in the Upper Big Branch disaster of 2010, claiming the lives of twenty-nine men, I am of the opinion that the company was in stark violation of the rule of law—not only of the safety rules so hard-won by the union but federal laws designed to establish a baseline of safety in the mines. The owners of UBB operated the mine with only one thought, mining a lot of coal. They refused to pay the numerous fines levied against them and thumbed their nose at federal regulators and mine safety inspectors. As I write this, a federal investigation has moved up the ladder of authority for the mine, gradually building a case against Massey Energy CEO Don Blankenship; he is not charged with is charged with conspiring to violate mine safety regulations and lying to securities regulators and investors after the tragedy. But the outcome is far from clear;

---

[5] As my son and I were completing this book the Lexington *Herald-Leader* newspaper reported that the last unionized mine in the state of Kentucky, where so much blood was shed fighting for the right to organize, had shut down; there is no longer a UMWA presence in the state. See "No union mines left in Kentucky, where labor wars once raged," September 6, 2015. The article goes on to note that "Union membership remains substantial in West Virginia, with more than 30,000 members, largely because that state wasn't affected by the environmental regulations on high-sulfur coal that essentially halted mining in western Kentucky in the 1990s."

verbally, he told his managers not to emphasize safety. Yet again and again he pushed them to dig more coal, more coal, and time and again denied requests for safety equipment and better ventilation. That he is on trial at all suggests that he's an outlier— the mines of West Virginia are an undeclared graveyard for miners whose owners talked the talk of safety, but walked the walk of profit. Fines for safety violations were so low that one of his subordinates testified that "It was cheaper to pay the fines than the cost of preventing violations." But if that's the case, and if the fines(even if paid) for not cleaning up a mine are less than the cost of cleaning up a mine, why shouldn't the mine owner choose the cheaper path? It comes down to a failure of political will, that states so reliant on coal, and a federal government that lurches between a hands-off policy and possible over-regulation of coal, can't find some common ground to protect the worker.

An explosion in a mine can be very small at its original ignition point, but the presence of gas and flammable coal dust can set off a chain reaction because of the wind current it creates in such a confined space. A spark can set the fine coal dust suspended in the air aflame, and the fire begins to feed on itself. Only an appropriate mixture of rock dust can keep the coal dust from igniting. A whole mine can become a shotgun barrel, with the explosion actually reaching from deep in the mine all the way to the drift mouth.

MEN BURIED 6 DAYS FOUND ALIVE IN MINE

Workers Entombed in Pennsylvania Colliery Crawl to Top of Chute to Escape Drowning.

TWO DAYS WITHOUT FOOD

One Saved Dinner Pail When Crash Came, Preventing Starvation of Prisoners—All Will Recover.

LANSFORD, Penn., Oct. 3.—The nine miners who were entombed last Monday in the Foster Creek tunnel of the Lehigh Coal and Navigation Company, at Coaldale, by a slide of coal dust, were taken out alive at 4:25 this afternoon. They were found on top of a chute in which they had crawled to escape a flood of water that had broken from an abandoned working and caused more than 300 feet of gangway roof to fall, shutting off means of escape. The men are now in the hospital, and reports from there tonight promise that all will recover. None of them, however, was in condition tonight to tell of their harrowing experience.

The rescued men are Elmer Herring, Peter Lermick, Joseph Murphy, John McAndrew, Dominick Holcheck, John Bononus, Michael Bodoidy, Joseph Lagonis, and Charles Matchakis. Two fellow-mine workers, William Watkins and George Holleywood, made their escape from the underground prison on Tuesday after crawling through holes made in the fallen rock and coal.

The rescue was accomplished after two hundred mine workers and company officials had battled for six days against discouraging conditions in the choked-up gangway. Their task was made more difficult by a three-foot stream of water which flowed from an adjoining working and which could be regulated only by the constant operation of many pumps.

After blasting and tearing away more than 300 feet of solid rock, coal, and timbers that had been wedged tightly into the gangway by the fall of the roof, rescue forces early today reached an open space, down which a stream of water poured from the undermined source. Once more their work was checked by the presence of an even deeper flow of water. A wooden platform resembling a large raft was built above the surface of the water, and the rescuers advanced toward the chutes where the entombed miners had taken refuge.

At the top of Chute No. 27, down which the coal from upper veins is thrown to the loading cars, the men were found huddled together. All were terribly weakened by their 150 hours' imprisonment, but when they saw the lights of the rescuers they hailed the party in weak voices.

The relatives and friends of the entombed men, who had been constantly at the mouth of the shaft since Monday, awaiting news from their beloved ones, did not know that the men were found until the first of the stretcher-bearers came out of the tunnel and lifted their burden into the ambulances. The report quickly spread, and soon 5,000 persons from the surrounding towns were gathered at the mine shaft.

Several of the rescued men talked cheerfully to their stretcher-bearers while being taken from the mine and from them it was learned that fish oil and a few crushed chicken bones had made up their principal diet until Thursday, when the latter "delicacy" gave out and the fish oil composition proved to be the only item on the bill of fare.

Each of the men had in his pockets several cakes of a fish oil substance that is used by mine workers in lamps and which gives a smokeless flame. One of them, John Bononus, saved his dinner pail when the slide occurred and this is probably what saved the men from starvation. In the pail Bononus had a large quantity of bread, other articles of food found in most miners' cans, and the greater portion of a roast chicken.

All of the food was shared among his companions, but the chicken was saved until the last. Not knowing how long they would be held prisoners, the men partook of their food in small quantities. For the past two days, however, they had been without food.

Everyone who has spent even a day mining coal knows the terrible thoughts that pass through one's mind as the mountain rumbles above them. Think of the Chilean miners. Some die instantly, some die slowly, and some survive, through a process of grace unknowable to mortals.

Each and every mine explosion leaves a trail of tears, memories and bitter resolve.

In July 1966 seven men were killed and two injured in an explosion at the Siltix mine in Mount Hope, where residents pass by this reminder every day.

The Sago mine disaster of 2006 cost the lives of twelve men, many of whom died after being entombed for nearly two days. Having spent so much time underground myself, I can clearly imagine their thoughts during those two days, having experienced many nightmares of being buried alive myself. I have carefully studied the various drawings that try to explain what went wrong at Sago. I wondered first why the mining company began another drift mouth so close to the old one.

It stands to reason that the older part of the original mine opening would have experienced neglect and lack of maintenance, and so a buildup of methane, water, and slate falls might be expected, cutting off ventilation to the old works. Another thing puzzling to me is, at the upper end of the drawing of the mine I've seen there's a turning point, but turning a breakthrough is usually on a 90-degree angle; the breakthrough for the newly mined section at Sago, near the site of the explosion, was at a much more obtuse angle. Is it possible this contributed to lack of proper ventilation?

According to the Mine Safety and Health Administration report about the accident, after the explosion the men retreated to a part of the mine where they knew there was adequate air. But there were many gaps in their barricade, which allowed poison gas into their refuge.

In mining the first rule is to secure the protective canvas very tightly to direct fresh air from the surface to where the miners are. If they had an adequate supply of timbers they could have used them a few feet apart to insure a tight curtain fit. But there are

During my career in the mines such headlines were not uncommon, and families waited long hours at the scene of a mine disaster for news of their loved ones.

always a lot of unanswered questions in any tragedy like this.

The proximate cause of the blast, according the post-blast studies, was lightning. I note that they said the lightning traveled through the ground until it made contact with a 1300-foot cable left in the old works. As an electrician, I know that lightning, like any electricity, seeks a ground. In the case of Sago, if there was no cable in the immediate vicinity, the lightning should have dissipated within a few yards of where it struck. However, I also note that the Sago mine—unlike Upper Big Branch—was sealed before an adequate and thorough investigation could be completed. One hates to think that a willingness to pursue a tragedy would wax and wane with the political climate, but the quality of the two investigations speak for themselves.

I can't help thinking of the reports that initially said the men had been found alive, but those stories had to be retracted to tell waiting families the bad news that all but one miner had perished. That's much worse than telling the families honestly that their loved ones died immediately. This indicates a lack of communication from outside to the farthest point the rescuers could reach.

At the Otsego mines the company had one man who was in charge of all telephone lines. He did a lot of crawling, of course, for the phone line ran along the wide walkway. When I first went into the mine in 1945 they had the old ringer phones which required lifting the receiver and cranking it up, such as you might see in an old war movie. I don't know exactly what communication system was in use at Sago so I won't assign blame for such miscommunication.

But in my mind I see widows who don't yet know they're widows and children who don't yet know they're orphans gathered around a makeshift barrel fire to await the news. They wait with dwindling hope.

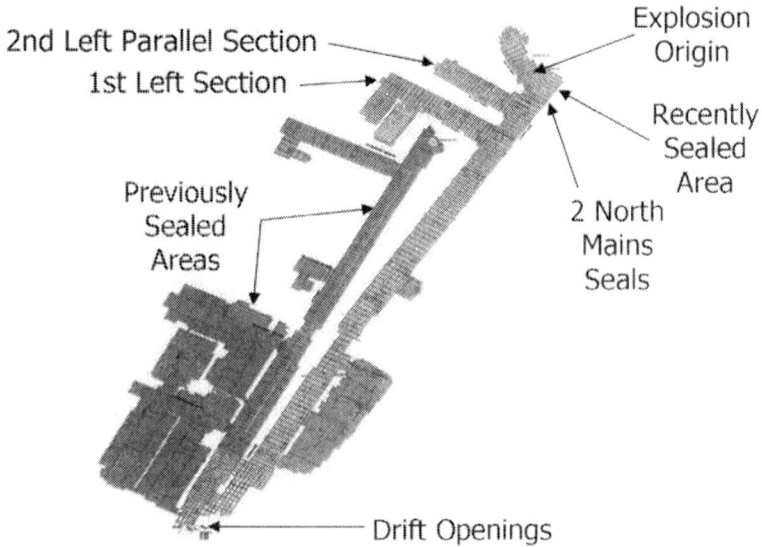

A schematic of the Sago mine at the time of the explosion.

The two explosions mentioned here are only footnotes to history. Blame may be assigned but it is never satisfying; possible reasons soon pass into the browning pages of a book read by fewer with each passing year. All that's left are the memories of brothers, fathers, grandfathers who died in the darkness.

Chapter 15 – Wear and Tear

By now, as the 1970's rolled on, I was beginning to show my age. War-related maladies that had lain semi-dormant for years began to reemerge. Though I had enjoyed this new kind of work in the shop it was sometimes hard, back-breaking work. My right knee was giving me a lot of trouble and at times when I was walking up or down steps my knee would lock up. One night when it did this I hopped around a couple hours, still doing my job, and asked Giles if I lay flat on the floor would he get hold of my foot and give it a jerk. He was hesitant.

I stuck my foot under the locomotive and reached back for something to hold on to. I took a deep breath and jerked hard as I could and heard my knee jump back into place. I just smiled at him and got up and walked away. There was, however, a lot of pain involved in this correction. At some point, I knew, the fix wouldn't be so simple.

One Sunday night I went to work even though I felt very bad. This often occurred but usually as I went to work it wore off. A month or so later, October, I went out as usual but with a different kind of sick feeling. I let my hanger down at the bathhouse and started to change into my work clothes. Suddenly I got very dizzy and almost passed out. I got my bag of clean work clothes into the basket and got the man next to me to pull it up. I made it back to my car OK and started it up.

From that point until I got home I don't remember anything, even passing through Mullens or parking the car at home. As I climbed the stairs I stumbled and fell. I cane to myself right then and wondered in my mind how I managed to drive twenty-five miles not knowing where I was.

The next day, after coming home sick, Recie drove me down to Rhodell to see Dr. Roberts. I always one to "wait my turn" so I wouldn't let Recie ask the doctor to see me. When they called the next patient she told the doctor that a very sick man was in the waiting room. The doctor came to the door, took one look at me, and sent her nurse out to get me and put me in bed. They began taking blood, urine and all kind of other samples. She gave me something to ease my pain and sent me home and said they would call as soon as the test results came in. I decided to take a few days off. The week following, my sister Nettie died and I got paid for those days and since it was Thanksgiving I also got holiday pay.

When I retired I literally hung up my hat—the helmet that had saved my life more than once.

When they called back in a few days I went back to see her and she began telling me what all they found lurking in my system. She told me my working days were over. I had depleted all my leave time I applied for my pension. On June 30, 1980 I went to the retirement office and told them I wished to retire. They then informed me I would have to go to Herndon to be separated, which I did, and by the time I returned to the retirement office it was four in the evening.

They filled out my papers and I looked at my watch. It was four-thirty in the evening. I was no longer a miner. On the drive home I felt a brief loneliness. So ended my life as a coal miner. The tropical diseases I acquired had come back and attacked my tired body. It was a sad day for me when I had to completely separate myself from the mining industry and it dawned on me that I was no longer a productive citizen, paying taxes and such. For a time really bothered me. Such is the life of a working man.

Now and then the coal mines come to me in dreams and I work just as hard in dreams as did in real time. Other times the war and work mingle and I perform dual duties. Though coal mining was and is a dangerous occupation there is a certain attraction to it. The sounds of it embed themselves into the soul and they, as do the war years, remain a part of a miner's life. A quiet time doing a simple repair job alone on a weekend leaves space for the sound of gas emitting from a coal seam like a swarm of bees, for the occasional crack of timbers taking on weight, the sound of a falling piece of roof in the distance.

But I got over it, as I contemplated the opportunities of a new way of life. The coal mine did not close down without me, nothing changed, and I began my retirement there in the coal mining town of Helen. My experience as a repairman, however, went on. I found out soon that many of the youth of the community knew me as a mechanic so when they had trouble of some kind they came to my work shop and asked me if I could fix it. A neighbor boy had a dirt bike with a bolt head broken off on the motor. His father couldn't fix it and his mom told him to see if Thurman could; if he can't, just forget it.

That reminded me of the time when the men couldn't get the bearing to go on. On the boy's bike I saw the size of the bolt and placed a smaller nut just above. Weighting the nut down I stuck my welding rod just above the nut, being careful not to move it. I filled the nut with weld and let it cool a minute and easily removed the broken bolt. A wide grin covered the boy's face.

Another boy came up with his four-wheeler and handle bar in four pieces. He asked if I could fix it. "Yeah," I said, "I can fix anything but a hole in the sky or a broken heart." He just laughed at that. I laid the broken pieces down and surveyed them. I had some three-eighths inch iron rod and proceeded to bend a piece just like the broken parts, which were hollow, and slid all of them into the handle bar. I checked it carefully and welded all of it together.

After satisfying myself that all the parts were strongly in place I ground off the rough places and spray-painted the bar. Next day he came by and he was very pleased. He asked how much he owed me and I told him not a thing. He told me if I ever need help to just let him know. Many times a boy came by with a low tire or some other little problem and word got around among the youth in Helen: "Take it to Thurman, he can fix it." For a child, you drop what you are doing and do whatever the child needs. Children came with all sorts of problems, school projects, and so on and still do. An eight-year-old did his school project based on a person my age, a sixteen-year-old came with a book to sign and purchased more, for he said he was deeply interested in the war I fought.

After I retired from the mines in 1980 the mining industry advanced far beyond my comprehension. For example, the "spad" was replaced by a laser beam. Old-fashioned starters were replaced by disposable circuit boards which made the use of blueprints virtually obsolete. When a component of a machine stopped, a whole printed circuit board was simply installed to correct the problem. I hated to see so much waste but understood the efficiency.

Chapter 16 – Homecoming

In later years Otsego has come to mean more to me. As I walked out of Cedar Creek into a life foreign to me I realized in later years that I had given five years of my life into another way of living, as a soldier. Many times, however, I would remember with pride the people I knew in Otsego, and the simple way of life that had now become so different.

When I was a child it was possible, especially on a moonlit night, for one to know exactly where he was relative to home and hearth by the contour of the mountains. For instance, where I grew up on Cedar Creek I could always look with wonder at three particular mountaintops as I rounded the curve leading to my home. I became a deep miner, but as I grew to manhood all around me I saw the consequences of extracting coal in a more profitable, but degrading, way.

Strip mining left huge highwalls which endangered animal life, hunters and domestic animals. Cows and horses often

Refuse from a mountaintop removal operation looms over a home, much as smoldering slate dumps surrounded many of the homes I lived in.

tumbled off these new high places and the scars left the hills with an ugly look. Now, mountaintop removal is even worse. Once the mountain tops are mined out the change is permanent. How far we've come—from mules and men shoveling coal by hand to mountaintop removal, where a "miner" can use his (or her) computer to operate the mining machine, resulting in thousands of jobs becoming obsolete. The argument is still that "coal provides jobs"—where are they? Meanwhile, as of this writing, in late 2015, the number of people employed in the solar power industry is greater than those employed in coal mining. I suspect that trend will not reverse.

The profits gained come as the coal is shipped out of state and then out of the U.S., but mountain people are left with only a memory of the hills of their youth. Between the towns of Otsego and Caloric there was a railroad tunnel and near Caloric there was a long cut of several hundred feet in the mountain. A long, wide swampy area lay just up from the cut and the coal companies began filling it with the rock leftover after the burnable coal was washed, commonly called coal refuse, thus filling the cut with a "slate pile." The pile was solid, like a rock pile, and you could walk on it. But such coal refuse still contains burnable material, just not of sufficient quality to produce heat without a lot of smoke. This slate pile ignited, due either to spontaneous

When a mine was played out the drift mouth and other openings should be sealed, since many a curious child has wandered into them and never come out. This driftmouth is in Mount Hope.

combustion or by someone kindling a fire. This set the entire slate pile to burning, creating a dangerous buildup of carbon monoxide. Several hobos, unaware of the danger, sought warmth on top of the pile in cold weather, and settled down to sleep, never to awaken. Smoldering or outright burning slate piles were common throughout southern West Virginia well into the 1970's.

After moving to Helen in 1957 we had to order coal from the company and hire it hauled to us. Sometimes the coal would have a lot of bone in it and consequently formed a lot of "clinkers." But the coal company at Helen had a mine up "first hollow," just below where we lived, and they made a large slate dump along the mountainside. Many times was a lot of good coal stuck to the rock; I took a hatchet and acquired a lot of free, pure coal that would otherwise have gone to waste that way.

Even where the mountains retain their natural contours they are often obscured by the ugly black leftovers of the mining process. There was a huge slate pile just above Helen. I sat many hours on my porch just looking up at that ugly scar. One day reclaimers began to rid the mountain of it.

The reclamation force brought a bulldozer up and began working on the slate dump. From my porch it looked like a little bug crawling around. Long after the work was done my son David and his son, Andrew, then about eight, climbed up to the top of the reclaimed mountain, which overlooked all of Helen. I also have 8mm movies taken from up there long before they reclaimed it, and we combined them and decided to name the reclaimed hill "Andrew's Mountain."

Throughout the Appalachian coal fields there were and are numerous such dumps, some along highways and some in secluded hollows. Many eventually caught fire due to spontaneous combustion. Once afire they were virtually impossible to extinguish.

When an entire dump had burned all its combustible material it turned a copperish red, which come to be called "red dog." Many people brought their pickup trucks and dump trucks and hauled a lot of it home for road repair. One company went into business making blocks, similar to cinder blocks, still retaining their reddish hue. The former slate dump above Helen now has huge rocks from the bottom to the top, forming a way for water to run through to prevent further erosion. And nature has a way, with a little help from man, of regaining some of its former splendor. Along the road into Stotesbury there is one now almost back to nature's green.

I only saw my father, Eli Center Miller, cry twice. The first was when he was told his son, Gilbert, had been killed in Florida. The only other time was in 1956 when we were forced to leave Cedar Creek, with just a few weeks' notice and nowhere else to go. He told me it was not so much the leaving but that he was unable to do it for himself. I remember well telling him, "You're not alone, Dad."

Now, as I approach the age of ninety-six, those years on Cedar Creek, among a bounty that no longer exists, are precious to me. Living outside the town on the farm, working with my parents, and delivering milk and fresh produce—thinking of these brings me back to my youth. Many times my dreams center on that early life.

But the five years of my Marine Corps life have embedded in my mind forever. Some things cannot be erased with age. Nine particular months of those five years invade my mind still. August through November and January through April come back to haunt me, the anniversaries of different battles, and I think more often of my comrades who never came home.

But I well remember when asked where in West Virginia I came from it was always: Otsego. I had a schoolteacher—Granny Delp— imbued with wisdom far in advance of her years. She taught her students the facts of life there at Otsego, even down to how to shake hands and how to greet our elders, how we should view the meaning of our Maker. Now in my retirement years these memories of a coal town remain and I cherish the memory of that life.

One day my son Gilbert and I went to look around where our Cedar Creek house stood just above Otsego until we had to move when he was ten. We found a gate where the old schoolhouse once stood, now the site of several homes. A man stepped out of his house and asked where did we think—yes, "think"—we were going? I told him and he said we couldn't go to our old home place. "Yeah?" I replied. "You going to stop us?"

We went around the gate and continued up to Gilbert's first home, my real home, on Cedar Creek.

The End

Appendix: Driving the Winding Gulf

Mullens and the other small cities near my hometown, such as this one of Welch in 1946, are more or less ghost towns now, with few people and little industry. It's difficult to convey how vibrant and bustling those towns were at one time, when abundant coal jobs provided a relatively comfortable near-middle class life and cities could support several movie theaters, a taxi service, many clothing shops, and so on. The Pocahontas Theater was famous in its day, beautifully appointed and costing $100,000 when it opened in 1928. See http://www.wvculture.org/history/entertainment/pocahontastheater01.html

The numerous coal towns shown on the maps in the Illustrations section above were active and vibrant as I grew up. The Winding Gulf was referred to as the "Billion Dollar Coalfield" for the depth and richness of its coal reserves. Yet the small towns that grew up literally above the coal are almost entirely gone, abandoned after the local mine played out. Though I did not travel extensively along these towns until in my early teens, I want to list them here and consider how they came to be named. Otsego is my hometown—or rather the left fork of Cedar Creek just above it—but Mullens is my reference point because its paved roads and bus and train service led me to the larger world. The Price brothers maintained a bus service from Mullens to Beckley and I used this many times from the late thirties until I could afford my own car, as many miners began to be able to do, and the bus line closed down.

Welch today.

From Mullens up Route 54 the journey takes us up Slab Fork Creek, past Nutria, Caloric, and Otsego. Slab Creek played a major role in my life growing up; unlike now, it then flowed relatively clean. I fished a lot in the Slab. I also delivered milk and, in the spring, garden veggies to the colored families living above the Slab Fork tipple.

There were numerous swimming holes along Slab and I swam in most of them. Caloric and Otsego are connected to my family, as my great- grandfather, Franklin Sizemore, first cleared the land upon which these were built. Next come Pierpoint and Maben. Maben was a town with dual economic bases, in that it was a coal town as well as a lumber center where Ritter Lumber maintained a huge sawmill. My brother Buck worked there for a time.

Of perhaps historic interest, this sawmill burned in the late thirties. That same evening, in the Otsego schoolhouse, a Pentecostal preacher was holding a revival. As the huge mill burned it lit up the sky even down to Otsego and could be seen for miles. Everyone in the schoolhouse came out to watch and many said it must be the start of the end of time.

After I came home from the war, my Dad started building a house for us just a ways above his home. Lumber, dry wall and any other building material was hard to come by then and I learned there was much lumber salvaged from the mill available. I bought enough of this lumber to floor my Cedar Creek home.

On next to Slab Fork. Listed as my place of birth, this town was a major coal producer back then and is still a neatly maintained little town, with the Virginian Railroad trestle still a dominant feature of the landscape. My cousins, the sons of William O. and Mandy Rinehart Whitt, worked there, one as the mine foreman and one as an electrician.

Next we come to Lester. This town was a shopping area, supplying mines at Glen White, Maple Meadow and Big Stick.

If we start again at Mullens but journey up what was called "The Gulf," or Route 16, we first encounter Black Eagle and Allen Junction, with Wyco just off the highway. There are still many houses in Wyco. In these coal towns the houses which have been maintained looking either partially or, rarely, wholly like the original miners' dwelling. Miners who chose to remain and those who later purchased these homes, as I did in Helen, remodeled them to suit their taste and covered the old paint with siding or other material. While still maintaining the original shape of the houses this made the community look neater.

We reach Iroquois, an Indian name, and then Stephenson and Amigo with Malcolm as an offshoot. Amigo stands at the dividing line between Raleigh and Wyoming Counties. This town has also maintained much of its identity even though there is no coal industry, with its portals and preparation plants, nearby. Amigo is also the confluence of Winding Gulf Creek and Stonecoal Creek and they combine to form the Guyandotte.

The Helen Miners' Memorial. Photo courtesy Carol Cadle.

Just north of Amigo is where the historic Byrd Prilliman School stood, and a quarter mile beyond that is Rhodell off to the east. A few miles further on Route 16 comes Helen, where I lived for almost fifty years. Helen is the only town along the Coal Heritage Trail which has kept itself up very well, while still maintaining much of its original identity as a coal camp. I recall visiting my brothers Gilbert and Kermit when I was a teenager during the thirties and hearing them talk of hauling coal around the mountain above and left of Helen. I called John Lewis, knowing he was a lifelong resident of Helen, and posed a few questions. He began telling me of various mine openings upon the mountain and described one almost up to the town of Ury on the left side of the mountain with a narrow-gauge haulage track which used with a small locomotive pulling small coal-loaded cars.

It dawned on me that my two brothers were the operators of this little mine, Gilbert and his brakeman, Kermit.

My half-brother Gilbert, for whom my oldest son is named, shown here with the brakeman who accompanied him on his last, fatal train ride in Florida.

This was a part of the many openings which the same coal company seam had at Stotesbury where they lived when I visited. John told me they pulled the cars out with mules. The company had day shift and night shift mules and when not being used they were confined to a large section of the woods surrounded by a wire fence.

A mile north of Helen is Ury (Cooktown) which existed as a very small but booming little town during the heyday of coal. We shortly come to Tams. Whereas Helen is laid out on both sides of the main road, and lies at the end of a very long and straight near-mile stretch between it and Ury, it was more open and people could come and go.

Not in Tams. Tams lay in the valley just to the east of Route

16, with a single road into the town. If anything happened in Tams, its benevolent owner, one of the last of the old coal barons, would know about it immediately. (In fact, I didn't discover until recently that much of what I considered part of Helen or Ury, or some unincorporated no-man's land, was actually owned by Tams—his property extended all the way to the backyards of the northernmost residents of Helen and included its baseball field.)

Lynn Knapp Walters has written an extensive account of Major W. P. Tams and the town that bore his name—her family lived in Tams during its glory days. She writes:

Mules were an expensive and well-treated resource in the early days of mining. Miners were easily replaceable, mules less so.

That little camp in the holler up on the Winding Gulf watershed was confined between rapidly rising rocky outcroppings and a thick mix of rhododendron, honeysuckle, oak, hemlock and maple under which copperheads slithered, but it had a big reach. Coal from Tams' mine went all the way to the nation's largest steel mills and U.S. Navy ships. […] Tams was known as a demanding taskmaster, yet benevolent dictator. He only offered redemption once, telling troublemakers to collect their things during a second run-in. "There's a saying around here that 'Anyone can see Mr. Tams,' but it is also commonly understood that the man who has run this million-dollar-a-year industry for 37 years "don't stand for no foolishness," wrote a reporter for the local Raleigh Register newspaper in 1947.

... He even presided over domestic disputes. If a husband and wife were arguing and yelling at each other, the constable Tams hired to patrol the streets of Tams would bring the couple to the Major, and he would settle the dispute, said West Virginia historian Ronald Eller. Yet, Tams could be unstintingly generous. "The aged and the lame are not forgotten men here.... 'As

The legendary Major W.P. Tams.

men become older and more disabled, the Major always makes a place for them, at something they can do,' one man explained."

... Tams, who shared so many similarities with the other early independent coal operators, diverged with them on certain key traits. He, too, came from outside the mountains, was well educated, and looking to make his fortune. These young bucks knew this chance to grab the brass ring didn't require a huge outlay of capital. For an initial investment of $20,000 to $30,000, they could haul millions out of the mountains. Yet, unlike the others, he didn't take the money and

FIRST COAL CAR SHIPPED IN 1909 FROM GULF CO.

Virginian First Served As Mining Engineer With Sam Dixon

By DICK MASON

The story of a man — Major W. P. Tams, Jr., — tells the story of one Raleigh County mining community, for probably no town in the world portrays so accurately the lengthened shadow of one man's personality as does this one on Winding Gulf Creek in the heart of the county's smokeless coal fields.

The Tams family, originally from Augusta County, Virginia, had been investors in the coal business since 1888. When the late Harry Frazier, Major Tams' uncle, obtained him a position as mining engineer with the late Sam Dixon, pioneer Fayette-Raleigh coal operator, he left the Seaboard Air-line Railway and came to Fayette County in 1904.

Forty-four years ago, Major Tams climbed on a horse at Mac-Donald and headed into the wilderness region along Winding Gulf Creek and Stonecoal to begin his exploration of that section of Raleigh County. After following a wagon road from Beckley to Sophia, the young mining engineer traveled a horse trail through the virgin timberland where his mine now stands to prospect for coal.

First Reaction

His reaction as he topped the crest of the hill and looked down into Winding Gulf Creek:

"Words could never adequately describe this beautiful natural scene of acre after acre of virgin timberland."

run.... William Purviance Tams, Jr., would be the first mine owner to drop hours in the work week from 10 to nine hours with no cut in pay in the winter of 1911, ahead of his peers, in a bid to ward off union organizers. That move bought him more than 20 years of union-free labor for the 300 to 400 men who dug black diamonds out of the hillside for his Gulf Smokeless Coal Company, first in the Beckley seam and then in the Pocahontas No. 4. The change also allowed miners precious daylight from their subterranean norm, which they often entered at 6 a.m., if not before. This southern gentleman was the first to introduce a motion picture theatre in 1911 to southern West Virginia miners and their families, who eventually totaled more than 1,000 in the isolated little community of Tams. The Raleigh Register, the local newspaper, wrote in 1917, some eight years after the first railroad car of coal shipped from the Tams mine that "The motion picture house is a credit to a town much larger than Tams." The recreation didn't stop there, although segregation was strictly enforced. "Separate amusement houses are maintained, one for

142

the colored people and one for the whites. They contain reading rooms, gymnasium, swimming pool, billiard and pool rooms, bowling alley, etc., together with a café in connection." Tams was also the first to provide a miner bathhouse to wash away the oily black grime that crept into every pore often defeating even the most fastidious of men.   The 1917 local newspaper article boasted the "change houses were the most modern and unique to be found anywhere, being designed by Mr. Tams himself for their convenience and perfect arrangement." A unique pulley-chain system lifted each man's grimy work clothes to the bathhouse ceiling for airing. A lock kept the clothes secure until the miner's return the next day. The same painstaking attention that Tams paid to his town he devoted to his mines. He personally inspected the mines, first No.1, then No. 2, 3, 4 and 5, demanding a zero tolerance for safety violations… "No man who has seen ever seen an explosion can be callous about human life,' said Tams in a voice rich with feeling during the Playboy interview." Tams related to the reporter his experience of witnessing a mine explosion firsthand in January 1907. The Stuart, W.V., mine blast killed 56 workers, including three 12-year-old boys. The experience made Tams "an abnormally cautious man." …Tams insisted on perfection in his mining operations. "If all was not perfect on his inspection tour, he issued immediate orders to set things right. He might well be back at four the next morning and woe be it if his commands had not been carried out to the letter." As a result, Tams operated his large-scale mining activities for more than 40 years without major loss of life. Yet, his mine claimed the life of the one person he held dearest, his only brother.

Raleigh Register

Major W. P. Tams Dead At Age 94

… His improvements were not totally altruistic. Tams had a drive to create something larger than him. Being first, in control, and the best were steps toward fulfilling his destiny. The benefits he provided miners and their families were also tactical steps to head off union organizers. Digging coal in southern West Virginia often provoked bitter labor disputes. Hot heads and quick triggers proved an explosive mix. Tams had felt the sting of not being able to persuade his fellow owners to forgo the bullying Pinkerton guards in the early 1900s. He'd been outvoted then, and bloody violence ensued as Mother Jones could testify. That's why he hadn't asked permission when he cut the workday length, and in effect, raised wages. He did it again a couple years later. Let the other owners wail about it after the fact. And, indeed, the steps he took rocked a world where the owners' word was law.

I have eliminated her footnotes in the above for readability, but encourage the reader to seek out her work.

All these towns at that time seemed to comprise one single community and in some cases it was hard to determine where one ended and the other began, all inhabited by coal miners with the same kinds of problems, about which everyone knew. There was a unity, and a community, in the coal field.

However, based as it was on a single source of income, it was a fragile community. Roul Tunley, writing in the February 6, 1960, edition of the *Saturday Evening Post*, called it "The Strange Case of West Virginia: Although rich in resources and natural beauty, the Mountain State suffers from chronic, grinding poverty. A report on an American paradox."

Tunley noted although the mining industry was very profitable, little of those profits reached the average West Virginian. The beautiful Greenbrier resort lies just a few hills away from communities of appalling squalor and deep poverty. Tunley visited Stotesbury as well as McAlpin. The entire article is worth reading, as it captures the many contradictions that define West Virginia. Tunley called Stotesbury an "unbelievably dismal ghost town," writing that he found

> rows of empty, decaying, grimy houses. Here and there a family still occupied an unpainted shack, surrounded by rubbish, weeds and soot. Overstuffed couches, their entrails bursting through the rags that covered them, sat sadly on the porches. Several children, their faces dirty, played silently in the empty streets. There was little activity anywhere, and less hope. One house showed some signs of life, and I stopped to investigate. There were five persons living in it—an elderly woman and her four grandchildren. The oldest child was a pretty blond girl of fifteen. She was the head of the family. She explained that the mine hadn't operated in two years, but since her parents had bought the house from the company for $1700, they had continued to live in it. With no money to repair it, the house, like all the others, was rotting away. It had four rooms, outdoor plumbing and few conveniences. The father had tried to get work elsewhere and had managed to do so for a time. But finally his luck ran out. He had taken his last relief check, put some gas in the family jalopy and, with his wife, gone to Cleveland to look for work. "As soon as daddy gets a job," said the girl, "we're all going to Cleveland." McAlpin. Stotesbury's neighbor, presents the other side of the bituminous coin. The mine is still operating, and although the community is far from attractive by even the loosest standards, it is still alive. The Testermans, whom I visited, are typical

of a working miner's family. They live in a company-owned frame house- "five rooms and path" is the way Mrs. Testerman put it—for which they pay only $15.20 a month. They have four children, and Fred Testerman, who is thirty-three, has never been unemployed. At present he works on a conveyor belt. Despite full employment for people like Fred Testerman, however, McAlpin is not a happy place. Too many people see the handwriting on the wall. They do not know when increasing mechanization of the mine will take their jobs away or when the mine will be found obsolete and closed down. They've seen it happen in Stotesbury and they know it can happen in McAlpin."

The photo of a Stotesbury family that accompanied Tunley's famous, or infamous, article. His portrait of West Virginia as mired in poverty remains unfortunately accurate to this day, despite all the coal that left the state over the years and her abundant natural resources and beauty.

And it did happen in McAlpin, and in every other small town that depended on coal as its only source of work—there was literally no other way to make a living, and when the mine was gone, so too was the mining town.

But that isn't the Stotesbury I knew as a child. The one I knew fell victim to what anthropologist Kathleen Stewart, writing in 1996, described as the "dizzying swings of boom and bust, the mechanization of the mines, the mass migrations of the fifties and sixties, the final boom during the oil crisis, the final mine closings in the eighties, the collapse of the place, the painful hanging on, the unthinkable leavings. Imagine how the place became a migrational space that caught people in the repetition of drifting back and forth from the hills to the cities looking for work... "[6]

---

[6] Stewart, K. 1996 *A Space by the Side of the Road: Cultural poetics in an 'other' America*. Princeton NJ: Princeton University Press

Glossary of Mining Terms
Courtesy www.coaleducation.org

Abutment - In coal mining, (1) the weight of the rocks above a narrow roadway is transferred to the solid coal along the sides, which act as abutments of the arch of strata spanning the roadway; and (2) the weight of the rocks over a longwall face is transferred to the front abutment, that is, the solid coal ahead of the face and the back abutment, that is, the settled packs behind the face.

Acid rain – Refers loosely to a mixture of wet and dry "deposition" (deposited material) from the atmosphere containing higher than "normal" amount of nitric and sulfuric acids. The precursors or chemical forerunners of acid rain formation result from both natural sources, such as volcanoes and decaying vegetation, and man-made sources, primarily emissions of sulfur and nitrogen oxides resulting from fossil fuel combustion.

Acid mine water - Mine water that contains free sulfuric acid, mainly due to the weathering of iron pyrites.

Active workings - Any place in a mine where miners are normally required to work or travel and which are ventilated and inspected regularly.

Adit - A nearly horizontal passage from the surface by which a mine is entered and dewatered. A blind horizontal opening into a mountain, with only one entrance.

Advance - Mining in the same direction, or order of sequence; first mining as distinguished from retreat.

Air split - The division of a current of air into two or more parts.

Airway - Any passage through which air is carried. Also known as an air course.

Anemometer - Instrument for measuring air velocity.

Angle of dip - The angle at which strata or mineral deposits are inclined to the horizontal plane.

Angle of draw - In coal mine subsidence, this angle is assumed to bisect the angle between the vertical and the angle of repose of the material and is 20° for flat seams. For dipping seams, the angle of break increases, being 35.8° from the vertical for a 40° dip. The main break occurs over the seam at an angle from the vertical equal to half the dip.

Angle of repose - The maximum angle from horizontal at which a given material will rest on a given surface without sliding or rolling.

Anticline - An upward fold or arch of rock strata.

Aquifer - A water-bearing bed of porous rock, often sandstone.

Arching - Fracture processes around a mine opening, leading to stabilization by an arching effect.

Area (of an airway) - Average width multiplied by average height of airway, expressed in square feet.

Auger - A rotary drill that uses a screw device to penetrate, break, and then transport the drilled material (coal).

Auxiliary operations - All activities supportive of but not contributing directly to mining.

Auxiliary ventilation - Portion of main ventilating current directed to face of dead end entry by means of an auxiliary fan and tubing.

Azimuth - A surveying term that references the angle measured clockwise from any meridian (the established line of reference). The bearing is used to designate direction. The bearing of a line is the acute horizontal angle between the meridian and the line.

Back - The roof or upper part in any underground mining cavity.

Backfill – Mine waste or rock used to support the roof after coal removal.

Barren - Said of rock or vein material containing no minerals of value, and of strata without coal, or containing coal in seams too thin to be workable.

Barricading - Enclosing part of a mine to prevent inflow of noxious gasses from a mine fire or an explosion.

Barrier - Something that bars or keeps out. Barrier pillars are solid blocks of coal left between two mines or sections of a mine to prevent accidents due to inrushes of water, gas, or from explosions or a mine fire.

Beam - A bar or straight girder used to support a span of roof between two support props or walls.

Beam building - The creation of a strong, inflexible beam by bolting or otherwise fastening together several weaker layers. In coal mining this is the intended basis for roof bolting.

Bearing – A surveying term used to designate direction. The bearing of a line is the acute horizontal angle between the meridian and the line. The meridian is an established line of reference. Azimuths are angles measured clockwise from any meridian.

Bearing plate - A plate used to distribute a given load. In roof bolting, the plate used between the bolt head and the roof.

Bed - A stratum of coal or other sedimentary deposit.

Belt conveyor - A looped belt on which coal or other materials can be carried and which is generally constructed of flame-resistant material or of reinforced rubber or rubber-like substance.

Belt idler - A roller, usually of cylindrical shape, which is supported on a frame and which, in turn, supports or guides a conveyor belt. Idlers are not powered but turn by contact with the moving belt.

Belt take-up - A belt pulley, generally under a conveyor belt and in by the drive pulley, kept under strong tension parallel to the belt line. Its purpose is to automatically compensate for any slack in the belting created by start-up, etc.

Bench - One of two or more divisions of a coal seam separated by slate or formed by the process of cutting the coal.

Beneficiation - The treatment of mined material, making it more concentrated or richer.

Berm - A pile or mound of material capable of restraining a vehicle.

Binder - A streak of impurity in a coal seam.

Bit - The hardened and strengthened device at the end of a drill rod that transmits the energy of breakage to the rock. The size of the bit determines the size of the hole. A bit may be either detachable from or integral with its supporting drill rod.

Bituminous coal – A middle rank coal (between subbituminous and anthracite) formed by additional pressure and heat on lignite. Usually has a high Btu value and may be referred to as "soft coal."

Black damp - A term generally applied to carbon dioxide. Strictly speaking, it is a mixture of carbon dioxide and nitrogen. It is also applied to an atmosphere depleted of oxygen, rather than having an excess of carbon dioxide.

Blasting agent - Any material consisting of a mixture of a fuel and an oxidizer.

Blasting cap - A detonator containing a charge of detonating compound, which is ignited by electric current or the spark of a fuse. Used for detonating explosives.

Blasting circuit - Electric circuits used to fire electric detonators or to ignite an igniter cord by means of an electric starter.

Bleeder or bleeder entries - Special air courses developed and maintained as part of the mine ventilation system and designed to continuously move air-methane mixtures emitted by the gob or at the active face away from the active workings and into mine-return air courses. Alt: Exhaust ventilation lateral.

Bolt torque - The turning force in foot-pounds applied to a roof bolt to achieve an installed tension.

Borehole - Any deep or long drill-hole, usually associated with a diamond drill.

Bottom - Floor or underlying surface of an underground excavation.

Boss - Any member of the managerial ranks who is directly in charge of miners (e.g., "shift-boss," "face-boss," "fire-boss," etc.).

Box-type magazine - A small, portable magazine used to store limited quantities of explosives or detonators for short periods of time at locations in the mine which are convenient to the blasting sites at which they will be used.

Brattice or brattice cloth - Fire-resistant fabric or plastic partition used in a mine passage to confine the air and force it into the working place. Also termed "line brattice," "line canvas," or "line curtain."

Break line - The line that roughly follows the rear edges of coal pillars that are being mined. The line along which the roof of a coal mine is expected to break.

Breakthrough - A passage for ventilation that is cut through the pillars between rooms.

Bridge carrier - A rubber-tire-mounted mobile conveyor, about 10 meters long, used as an intermediate unit to create a system of articulated conveyors between a mining machine and a room or entry conveyor.

Bridge conveyor - A short conveyor hung from the boom of mining or lading machine or haulage system with the other end attached to a receiving bin that dollies along a frame supported by the room or entry conveyor, tailpiece. Thus, as the machine boom moves, the bridge conveyor keeps it in constant connection with the tailpiece.

Brow - A low place in the roof of a mine, giving insufficient headroom.

Brushing - Digging up the bottom or taking down the top to give more headroom in roadways.

Btu – British thermal unit. A measure of the energy required to raise the temperature of one pound of water one degree Fahrenheit.

Bug dust - The fine particles of coal or other material resulting from the boring or cutting of the coal face by drill or machine.

Bump (or burst) - A violent dislocation of the mine workings which is attributed to severe stresses in the rock surrounding the workings.

Butt cleat - A short, poorly defined vertical cleavage plane in a coal seam, usually at right angles to the long face cleat.

Butt entry - A coal mining term that has different meanings in different locations. It can be synonymous with panel entry, submain entry, or in its older sense it refers to an entry that is "butt" onto the coal cleavage (that is, at right angles to the face).

Cage - In a mine shaft, the device, similar to an elevator car, that is used for hoisting personnel and materials.

Calorific value - The quantity of heat that can be liberated from one pound of coal or oil measured in BTU's.

Cannel coal - A massive, non-caking block coal with a fine, even grain and a conchoidal fracture which has a high percentage of hydrogen, burns with a long, yellow flame, and is extremely easy to ignite.

Canopy - A protective covering of a cab on a mining machine.

Cap - A miner's safety helmet. Also, a highly sensitive, encapsulated explosive that is used to detonate larger but less sensitive explosives.

Cap block - A flat piece of wood inserted between the top of the prop and the roof to provide bearing support.

Car - A railway wagon, especially any of the wagons adapted to carrying coal, ore, and waste underground.

Car-dump - The mechanism for unloading a loaded car.

Carbide bit - More correctly, cemented tungsten carbide. A cutting or drilling bit for rock or coal, made by fusing an insert of molded tungsten carbide to the cutting edge of a steel bit shank.

Cast - A directed throw; in strip-mining, the overburden is cast from the coal to the previously mined area.

Certified - Describes a person who has passed an examination to do a required job.

Chain conveyor - A conveyor on which the material is moved along solid pans (troughs) by the action of scraper crossbars attached to powered chains.

Chain pillar - The pillar of coal left to protect the gangway or entry and the parallel airways.

Check curtain - Sheet of brattice cloth hung across an airway to control the passage of the air current.

Chock - Large hydraulic jacks used to support roof in longwall and shortwall mining systems.

Clay vein - A body of clay-like material that fills a void in a coal bed.

Cleat - The vertical cleavage of coal seams. The main set of joints along which coal breaks when mined.

Clean Air Act Amendments of 1990 – A comprehensive set of amendments to the federal law governing the nation's air quality. The Clean Air Act was originally passed in 1970 to address significant air pollution problems in our cities. The 1990 amendments broadened and strengthened the original law to address specific problems such as acid deposition, urban smog, hazardous air pollutants and stratospheric ozone depletion.

Clean Coal Technologies – A number of innovative, new technologies designed to use coal in a more efficient and cost-effective manner while enhancing environmental protection. Several promising technologies include: fluidized-bed combustion, integrated gasification combined cycle, limestone injection multi-stage burner, enhanced flue gas desulfurization (or "scrubbing"), coal liquefaction and coal gasification.

Coal - A solid, brittle, more or less distinctly stratified combustible carbonaceous rock, formed by partial to complete decomposition of vegetation; varies in color from dark brown to black; not fusible without decomposition and very insoluble.

Coal dust - Particles of coal that can pass a No. 20 sieve.

Coal Gasification – The conversion of coal into a gaseous fuel.

Coal mine - An area of land and all structures, facilities, machinery, tools, equipment, shafts, slopes, tunnels, excavations, and other property, real or personal, placed upon, under, or above the surface of such land by any person, used in extracting coal from its natural deposits in the earth by any means or method, and the work of preparing the coal so extracted, including coal preparation facilities. British term is "colliery".

Coal reserves - Measured tonnages of coal that have been calculated to occur in a coal seam within a particular property.

Coal washing – The process of separating undesirable materials from coal based on differences in densities. Pyritic sulfur, or sulfur combined with iron, is heavier and sinks in water; coal is lighter and floats.

Coke – A hard, dry carbon substance produced by heating coal to a very high temperature in the absence of air.

Collar - The term applied to the timbering or concrete around the mouth or top of a shaft. The beginning point of a shaft or drill hole at the surface.

Colliery - British name for coal mine.

Column flotation – A precombustion coal cleaning technology in which coal particles attach to air bubbles rising in a vertical column. The coal is then removed at the top of the column.

Comminution - The breaking, crushing, or grinding of coal, ore, or rock.

Competent rock - Rock which, because of its physical and geological characteristics, is capable of sustaining openings without any structural support except pillars and walls left during mining (stalls, light props, and roof bolts are not considered structural support).

Contact - The place or surface where two different kinds of rocks meet. Applies to sedimentary rocks, as the contact between a limestone and a sandstone, for example, and to metamorphic rocks; and it is especially applicable between igneous intrusions and their walls.

Continuous miner - A machine that constantly extracts coal while it loads it. This is to be distinguished from a conventional, or cyclic, unit which must stop the extraction process in order for loading to commence.

Contour - An imaginary line that connects all points on a surface having the same elevation.

Conventional mining – The first fully-mechanized underground mining method involving the insertion of explosives in a coal seam, the blasting of the seam, and the removal of the coal onto a conveyor or shuttle car by a loading machine.

Conveyor - An apparatus for moving material from one point to another in a continuous fashion. This is accomplished with an endless (that is, looped) procession of hooks, buckets, wide rubber belt, etc.

Core sample – A cylinder sample generally 1-5" in diameter drilled out of an area to determine the geologic and chemical analysis of the overburden and coal.

Cover - The overburden of any deposit.

Creep - The forcing of pillars into soft bottom by the weight of a strong roof. In surface mining, a very slow movement of slopes downhill.

Crib - A roof support of prop timbers or ties, laid in alternate cross-layers, log-cabin style. It may or may not be filled with debris. Also may be called a chock or cog.

Cribbing - The construction of cribs or timbers laid at right angles to each other, sometimes filled with earth, as a roof support or as a support for machinery.

Crop coal - Coal at the outcrop of the seam. It is usually considered of inferior quality due to partial oxidation, although this is not always the case.

Crossbar - The horizontal member of a roof timber set supported by props located either on roadways or at the face.

Crosscut - A passageway driven between the entry and its parallel air course or air courses for ventilation purposes. Also, a tunnel driven from one seam to another through or across the intervening measures; sometimes called "crosscut tunnel", or "breakthrough". In vein mining, an entry perpendicular to the vein.

Cross entry - An entry running at an angle with the main entry.

Crusher - A machine for crushing rock or other materials. Among the various types of crushers are the ball mill, gyratory crusher, Handsel mill, hammer mill, jaw crusher, rod mill, rolls, stamp mill, and tube mill.

Cutter; Cutting machine - A machine, usually used in coal, that will cut a 10- to 15-cm slot. The slot allows room for expansion of the broken coal. Also applies to the man who operates the machine and to workers engaged in the cutting of coal by prick or drill.

Cycle mining - A system of mining in more than one working place at a time, that is, a miner takes a lift from the face and moves to another face while permanent roof support is established in the previous working face.

Demonstrated reserves – A collective term for the sum of coal in both measured and indicated resources and reserves.

Deposit - Mineral deposit or ore deposit is used to designate a natural occurrence of a useful mineral, or an ore, in sufficient extent and degree of concentration to invite exploitation.

Depth - The word alone generally denotes vertical depth below the surface. In the case of incline shafts and boreholes it may mean the distance reached from the beginning of the shaft or hole, the borehole depth, or the inclined depth.

Detectors - Specialized chemical or electronic instruments used to detect mine gases.

Detonator - A device containing a small detonating charge that is used for detonating an explosive, including, but not limited to, blasting caps, exploders, electric detonators, and delay electric blasting caps.

Development mining - Work undertaken to open up coal reserves as distinguished from the work of actual coal extraction.

Diffusion - Blending of a gas and air, resulting in a homogeneous mixture. Blending of two or more gases.

Diffuser fan - A fan mounted on a continuous miner to assist and direct air delivery from the machine to the face.

Dilute - To lower the concentration of a mixture; in this case the concentration of any hazardous gas in mine air by addition of fresh intake air.

Dilution - The contamination of ore with barren wall rock in stopping.

Dip - The inclination of a geologic structure (bed, vein, fault, etc.) from the horizontal; dip is always measured downwards at right angles to the strike.

Dragline – A large excavation machine used in surface mining to remove overburden (layers of rock and soil) covering a coal seam. The dragline casts a wire rope-hung bucket a considerable distance, collects the dug material by pulling the bucket toward itself on the ground with a second wire rope (or chain), elevates the bucket, and dumps the material on a spoil bank, in a hopper, or on a pile.

Drainage - The process of removing surplus ground or surface water either by artificial means or by gravity flow.

Draw slate - A soft slate, shale, or rock from approximately 1 cm to 10 cm thick and located immediately above certain coal seams, which falls quite easily when the coal support is withdrawn.

Drift - A horizontal passage underground. A drift follows the vein, as distinguished from a crosscut that intersects it, or a level or gallery, which may do either.

Drift mine – An underground coal mine in which the entry or access is above water level and generally on the slope of a hill, driven horizontally into a coal seam.

Drill - A machine utilizing rotation, percussion (hammering), or a combination of both to make holes. If the hole is much over 0.4m in diameter, the machine is called a borer.

Drilling - The use of such a machine to create holes for exploration or for loading with explosives.

Dummy - A bag filled with sand, clay, etc., used for stemming a charged hole.

Dump - To unload; specifically, a load of coal or waste; the mechanism for unloading, e.g. a car dump (sometimes called tipple); or, the pile created by such unloading, e.g. a waste dump (also called heap, pile, tip, spoil pike, etc.).

Electrical grounding - To connect with the ground to make the earth part of the circuit.

Entry - An underground horizontal or near-horizontal passage used for haulage, ventilation, or as a mainway; a coal heading; a working place where the coal is extracted from the seam in the initial mining; same as "gate" and "roadway," both British terms.

Evaluation - The work involved in gaining a knowledge of the size, shape, position and value of coal.

Exploration - The search for mineral deposits and the work done to prove or establish the extent of a mineral deposit. Alt: Prospecting and subsequent evaluation.

Explosive - Any rapidly combustive or expanding substance. The energy released during this rapid combustion or expansion can be used to break rock.

Extraction - The process of mining and removal of coal or ore from a mine.

Face – The exposed area of a coal bed from which coal is being extracted.

Face cleat - The principal cleavage plane or joint at right angles to the stratification of the coal seam.

Face conveyor - Any conveyor used parallel to a working face which delivers coal into another conveyor or into a car.

Factor of safety - The ratio of the ultimate breaking strength of the material to the force exerted against it. If a rope will break under a load of 6000 lbs., and it is carrying a load of 2000 lbs., its factor of safety is 6000 divided by 2000 which equals 3.

Fall - A mass of roof rock or coal which has fallen in any part of a mine.

Fan, auxiliary - A small, portable fan used to supplement the ventilation of an individual working place.

Fan, booster - A large fan installed in the main air current, and thus in tandem with the main fan.

Fan signal - Automation device designed to give alarm if the main fan slows down or stops.

Fault - A slip-surface between two portions of the earth's surface that have moved relative to each other. A fault is a failure surface and is evidence of severe earth stresses.

Fault zone - A fault, instead of being a single clean fracture, may be a zone hundreds or thousands of feet wide. The fault zone consists of numerous interlacing small faults or a confused zone of gouge, breccia, or mylonite.

Feeder - A machine that feeds coal onto a conveyor belt evenly.

Fill - Any material that is put back in place of the extracted ore to provide ground support.

Fire damp - The combustible gas, methane, CH_4. Also, the explosive methane-air mixtures with between 5% and 15% methane. A combustible gas formed in mines by decomposition of coal or other carbonaceous matter, and that consists chiefly of methane.

Fissure - An extensive crack, break, or fracture in the rocks.

Fixed carbon – The part of the carbon that remains behind when coal is heated in a closed vessel until all of the volatile matter is driven off.

Flat-lying - Said of deposits and coal seams with a dip up to 5 degrees.

Flight - The metal strap or crossbar attached to the drag chain-and-flight conveyor.

Float dust - Fine coal-dust particles carried in suspension by air currents and eventually deposited in return entries. Dust consisting of particles of coal that can pass through a No. 200 sieve.

Floor - That part of any underground working upon which a person walks or upon which haulage equipment travels; simply the bottom or underlying surface of an underground excavation.

Flue Gas Desulfurization – Any of several forms of chemical/physical processes that remove sulfur compounds formed during coal combustion. The devices, commonly called "scrubbers," combine the sulfur in gaseous emissions with another chemical medium to form inert "sludge" which must then be removed for disposal.

Fluidized Bed Combustion – A process with a high degree of ability to remove sulfur from coal during combustion. Crushed coal and limestone are suspended in the bottom of a boiler by an upward stream of hot air. The coal is burned in this bubbling, liquid-like (or "fluidized") mixture. Rather than released as emissions, sulfur from combustion gases combines with the limestone to form a solid compound recovered with the ash.

Fly ash – The finely divided particles of ash suspended in gases resulting from the combustion of fuel. Electrostatic precipitators are used to remove fly ash from the gases prior to the release from a power plant's smokestack.

Formation – Any assemblage of rocks which have some character in common, whether of origin, age, or composition. Often, the word is loosely used to indicate anything that has been formed or brought into its present shape.

Fossil fuel – Any naturally occurring fuel of an organic nature, such as coal, crude oil and natural gas.

Fracture - A general term to include any kind of discontinuity in a body of rock if produced by mechanical failure, whether by shear stress or tensile stress. Fractures include faults, shears, joints, and planes of fracture cleavage.

Friable - Easy to break, or crumbling naturally. Descriptive of certain rocks and minerals.

Fuse - A cord-like substance used in the ignition of explosives. Black powder is entrained in the cord and, when lit, burns along the cord at a set rate. A fuse can be safely used to ignite a cap, which is the primer for an explosive.

Gallery - A horizontal or a nearly horizontal underground passage, either natural or artificial.

Gasification – Any of various processes by which coal is turned into low, medium, or high Btu gases.

Gathering conveyor; gathering belt - Any conveyor which is used to gather coal from other conveyors and deliver it either into mine cars or onto another conveyor. The term is frequently used with belt conveyors placed in entries where a number of room conveyors deliver coal onto the belt.

Geologist - One who studies the constitution, structure, and history of the earth's crust, conducting research into the formation and dissolution of rock layers, analyzing fossil and mineral content of layers, and endeavoring to fix historical sequence of development by relating characteristics to known geological influences (historical geology).

Gob - The term applied to that part of the mine from which the coal has been removed and the space more or less filled up with waste. Also, the loose waste in a mine. Also called goaf.

Global climate change – This term usually refers to the gradual warming of the earth caused by the greenhouse effect. Many scientists believe this is the result of man-made emissions of greenhouse gases such as carbon dioxide, chlorofluorocarbons (CFC) and methane, although there is no agreement among the scientific community on this controversial issue.

Grain - In petrology, that factor of the texture of a rock composed of distinct particles or crystals which depends upon their absolute size.

Grizzly - Course screening or scalping device that prevents oversized bulk material from entering a material transfer system; constructed of rails, bars, beams, etc.

Ground control - The regulation and final arresting of the closure of the walls of a mined area. The term generally refers to measures taken to prevent roof falls or coal bursts.

Ground pressure - The pressure to which a rock formation is subjected by the weight of the superimposed rock and rock material or by diastrophic forces created by movements in the rocks forming the earth's crust. Such pressures may be great enough to cause rocks having a low compressional strength to deform and be squeezed into and close a borehole or other underground opening not adequately strengthened by an artificial support, such as casing or timber.

Gunite - A cement applied by spraying to the roof and sides of a mine passage.

Haulage - The horizontal transport of ore, coal, supplies, and waste. The vertical transport of the same is called hoisting.

Haulageway - Any underground entry or passageway that is designed for transport of mined material, personnel, or equipment, usually by the installation of track or belt conveyor.

Headframe - The structure surmounting the shaft which supports the hoist rope pulley, and often the hoist itself.

Heading - A vein above a drift. An interior level or airway driven in a mine. In longwall workings, a narrow passage driven upward from a gangway in starting a working in order to give a loose end.

Head section - A term used in both belt and chain conveyor work to designate that portion of the conveyor used for discharging material.

Heaving - Applied to the rising of the bottom after removal of the coal; a sharp rise in the floor is called a "hogsback".

Highwall – The unexcavated face of exposed overburden and coal in a surface mine or in a face or bank on the uphill side of a contour mine excavation.

Highwall miner – A highwall mining system consists of a remotely controlled continuous miner which extracts coal and conveys it via augers, belt or chain conveyors to the outside. The cut is typically a rectangular, horizontal cut from a highwall bench, reaching depths of several hundred feet or deeper.

Hogsback - A sharp rise in the floor of a seam.

Hoist - A drum on which hoisting rope is wound in the engine house, as the cage or skip is raised in the hoisting shaft.

Hoisting - The vertical transport coal or material.

Horizon - In geology, any given definite position or interval in the stratigraphic column or the scheme of stratigraphic classification; generally used in a relative sense.

Horseback - A mass of material with a slippery surface in the roof; shaped like a horse's back.

Hydraulic - Of or pertaining to fluids in motion. Hydraulic cement has a composition which permits it to set quickly under water. Hydraulic jacks lift through the force transmitted to the movable part of the jack by a liquid. Hydraulic control refers to the mechanical control of various parts of machines, such as coal cutters, loaders, etc., through the operation or action of hydraulic cylinders.

Hydrocarbon – A family of chemical compounds containing carbon and hydrogen atoms in various combinations, found especially in fossil fuels.

Inby - In the direction of the working face.

Incline - Any entry to a mine that is not vertical (shaft) or horizontal (adit). Often incline is reserved for those entries that are too steep for a belt conveyor (+17 degrees -18 degrees), in which case a hoist and guide rails are employed. A belt conveyor incline is termed a slope. Alt: Secondary inclined opening, driven upward to connect levels, sometimes on the dip of a deposit; also called "inclined shaft".

Incompetent - Applied to strata, a formation, a rock, or a rock structure not combining sufficient firmness and flexibility to transmit a thrust and to lift a load by bending.

In situ - In the natural or original position. Applied to a rock, soil, or fossil when occurring in the situation in which it was originally formed or deposited.

Intake - The passage through which fresh air is drawn or forced into a mine or to a section of a mine.

Intermediate section - A term used in belt and chain conveyor network to designate a section of the conveyor frame occupying a position between the head and foot sections.

Immediate roof - The roof strata immediately above the coalbed, requiring support during the excavation of coal.

J

Jackleg - A percussion drill used for drifting or stopping that is mounted on a telescopic leg which has an extension of about 2.5 m. The leg and machine are hinged so that the drill need not be in the same direction as the leg.

Jackrock – A caltrop or other object manufactured with one or more rounded or sharpened points, which when placed or thrown present at least one point at such an angle that it is peculiar to and designed for use in puncturing or damaging vehicle tires. Jackrocks are commonly used during labor disputes.

Job Safety Analysis (J.S.A.) - A job breakdown that gives a safe, efficient job procedure.

Joint - A divisional plane or surface that divides a rock and along which there has been no visible movement parallel to the plane or surface.

Kettle bottom - A smooth, rounded piece of rock, cylindrical in shape, which may drop out of the roof of a mine without warning. The origin of this feature is thought to be the remains of the stump of a tree that has been replaced by sediments so that the original form has been rather well preserved.

Kerf - The undercut of a coal face.

Lamp - The electric cap lamp worn for visibility. Also, the flame safety lamp used in coal mines to detect methane gas concentrations and oxygen deficiency.

Layout - The design or pattern of the main roadways and workings. The proper layout of mine workings is the responsibility of the manager aided by the planning department.

Lift - The amount of coal obtained from a continuous miner in one mining cycle.

Liquefaction – The process of converting coal into a synthetic fuel, similar in nature to crude oil and/or refined products, such as gasoline.

Lithology - The character of a rock described in terms of its structure, color, mineral composition, grain size, and arrangement of its component parts; all those visible features that in the aggregate impart individuality of the rock. Lithology is the basis of correlation in coal mines and commonly is reliable over a distance of a few miles.

Load - To place explosives in a drill hole. Also, to transfer broken material into a haulage device.

Loading machine - Any device for transferring excavated coal into the haulage equipment.

Loading pocket - Transfer point at a shaft where bulk material is loaded by bin, hopper, and chute into a skip.

Longwall Mining – One of three major underground coal mining methods currently in use. Employs a steal plow, or rotation drum, which is pulled mechanically back and forth across a face of coal that is usually several hundred feet long. The loosened coal falls onto a conveyor for removal from the mine.

Loose coal - Coal fragments larger in size than coal dust.

Low voltage - Up to and including 660 volts by federal standards.

Main entry - A main haulage road. Where the coal has cleats, main entries are driven at right angles to the face cleats.

Main fan - A mechanical ventilator installed at the surface; operates by either exhausting or blowing to induce airflow through the mine roadways and workings.

Manhole - A safety hole constructed in the side of a gangway, tunnel, or slope in which miner can be safe from passing locomotives and car. Also called a refuge hole.

Man trip - A carrier of mine personnel, by rail or rubber tire, to and from the work area.

Manway - An entry used exclusively for personnel to travel form the shaft bottom or drift mouth to the working section; it is always on the intake air side in gassy mines. Also, a small passage at one side or both sides of a breast, used as a traveling way for the miner, and sometimes, as an airway, or chute, or both.

Measured coal resources – Coal for which estimates of the rank, quality, and quantity have been computed from sample analyses and measurements from closely spaced and geologically well-known sample sites, such as outcrops, trenches, mine workings, and drill holes. The points of observation and measurement are so closely spaced and the thickness and extent of coals are so well defined that the tonnage is judged to be accurate within 20 percent of true tonnage. Although the spacing of the points of observation necessary to demonstrate continuity of the coal differs from region to region according to the character of the coal beds, the points of observation are no greater than ½ mile apart. Measured coal is projected to extend as a ¼-mile wide belt from the outcrop or points of observation or measurement.

Meridian -– A surveying term that establishes a line of reference. The bearing is used to designate direction. The bearing of a line is the acute horizontal angle between the meridian and the line. Azimuths are angles measured clockwise from any meridian.

Methane – A potentially explosive gas formed naturally from the decay of vegetative matter, similar to that which formed coal. Methane, which is the principal component of natural gas, is frequently encountered in underground coal mining operations and is kept within safe limits through the use of extensive mine ventilation systems.

Methane monitor - An electronic instrument often mounted on a piece of mining equipment, that detects and measures the methane content of mine air.

Mine development - The term employed to designate the operations involved in preparing a mine for ore extraction. These operations include tunneling, sinking, cross-cutting, drifting, and raising.

Mine mouth electric plant – A coal burning electric-generating plant built near a coal mine.

Miner - One who is engaged in the business or occupation of extracting ore, coal, precious substances, or other natural materials from the earth's crust.

Mineral - An inorganic compound occurring naturally in the earth's crust, with a distinctive set of physical properties, and a definite chemical composition.

Mining Engineer - A person qualified by education, training, and experience in mining engineering. A trained engineer with knowledge of the science, economics, and arts of mineral location, extraction, concentration and sale, and the administrative and financial problems of practical importance in connection with the profitable conduct of mining.

Misfire - The complete or partial failure of a blasting charge to explode as planned.

MSHA - Mine Safety and Health Administration; the federal agency which regulates coal mine health and safety.

Mud cap - A charge of high explosive fired in contact with the surface of a rock after being covered with a quantity of wet mud, wet earth, or sand, without any borehole being used. Also termed adobe, dobie, and sandblast (illegal in coal mining).

Natural ventilation - Ventilation of a mine without the aid of fans or furnaces.

Nip - Device at the end of the trailing cable of a mining machine used for connecting the trailing cable to the trolley wire and ground.

Open end pillaring - A method of mining pillars in which no stump is left; the pockets driven are open on the gob side and the roof is supported by timber.

Outby; outbye - Nearer to the shaft, and hence farther from the working face. Toward the mine entrance. The opposite of inby.

Outcrop – Coal that appears at or near the surface.

Overburden – Layers of soil and rock covering a coal seam. Overburden is removed prior to surface mining and replaced after the coal is taken from the seam.

Overcast (undercast) - Enclosed airway which permits one air current to pass over (under) another without interruption.

Panel - A coal mining block that generally comprises one operating unit.

Panic bar - A switch, in the shape of a bar, used to cut off power at the machine in case of an emergency.

Parting - (1) A small joint in coal or rock; (2) a layer of rock in a coal seam; (3) a side track or turnout in a haulage road.

Peat – The partially decayed plant matter found in swamps and bogs, one of the earliest stages of coal formation.

Percentage extraction - The proportion of a coal seam which is removed from the mine. The remainder may represent coal in pillars or coal which is too thin or inferior to mine or lost in mining. Shallow coal mines working under townships, reservoirs, etc., may extract 50%, or less, of the entire seam, the remainder being left as pillars to protect the surface. Under favorable conditions, longwall mining may extract from 80 to 95% of the entire seam. With pillar methods of working, the extraction ranges from 50 to 90% depending on local conditions.

Percussion drill - A drill, usually air powered, that delivers its energy through a pounding or hammering action.

Permissible - That which is allowable or permitted. It is most widely applied to mine equipment and explosives of all kinds which are similar in all respects to samples that have passed certain tests of the MSHA and can be used with safety in accordance with specified conditions where hazards from explosive gas or coal dust exist.

Permit – As it pertains to mining, a document issued by a regulatory agency that gives approval for mining operations to take place.

Piggy-back - A bridge conveyor.

Pillar - An area of coal left to support the overlying strata in a mine; sometimes left permanently to support surface structures.

Pillar robbing - The systematic removal of the coal pillars between rooms or chambers to regulate the subsidence of the roof. Also termed "bridging back" the pillar, "drawing" the pillar, or "pulling" the pillar.

Pinch - A compression of the walls of a vein or the roof and floor of a coal seam so as to "squeeze" out the coal.

Pinch – A compression of the roof and floor of a coal seam so as to "squeeze" out the coal.

Pinning - Roof bolting.

Pitch - The inclination of a seam; the rise of a seam.

Plan - A map showing features such as mine workings or geological structures on a horizontal plane.

Pneumoconiosis - A chronic disease of the lung arising from breathing coal dust.

Portal - The structure surrounding the immediate entrance to a mine; the mouth of an adit or tunnel.

Portal bus - Track-mounted, self-propelled personnel carrier that holds 8 to 12 people.

Post - The vertical member of a timber set.

Preparation plant - A place where coal is cleaned, sized, and prepared for market.

Primary roof - The main roof above the immediate top. Its thickness may vary from a few to several thousand feet.

Primer (booster) - A package or cartridge of explosive which is designed specifically to transmit detonation to other explosives and which does not contain a detonator.

Prop - Coal mining term for any single post used as roof support. Props may be timber or steel; if steel—screwed, yieldable, or hydraulic.

Proximate analysis - A physical, or non-chemical, test of the constitution of coal. Not precise, but very useful for determining the commercial value. Using the same sample (1 gram) under controlled heating at fixed temperatures and time periods, moisture, volatile matter, fixed carbon and ash content are successfully determined. Sulfur and Btu content are also generally reported with a proximate analysis.

Pyrite - A hard, heavy, shiny, yellow mineral, FeS2 or iron disulfide, generally in cubic crystals. Also called iron pyrites, fool's gold, sulfur balls. Iron pyrite is the most common sulfide found in coal mines.

Raise - A secondary or tertiary inclined opening, vertical or near-vertical opening driven upward form a level to connect with the level above, or to explore the ground for a limited distance above one level.

Ramp - A secondary or tertiary inclined opening, driven to connect levels, usually driven in a downward direction, and used for haulage.

Ranks of coal – The classification of coal by degree of hardness, moisture and heat content. "Anthracite" is hard coal, almost pure carbon, used mainly for heating homes. "Bituminous" is soft coal. It is the most common coal found in the United States and is used to generate electricity and to make coke for the steel industry. "Subbituminous" is a coal with a heating value between bituminous and lignite. It has low fixed carbon and high percentages of volatile matter and moisture. "Lignite" is the softest coal and has the highest moisture content. It is used for generating electricity and for conversion into synthetic gas. In terms of Btu or "heating" content, anthracite has the highest value, followed by bituminous, subbituminous and lignite.

Reclamation – The restoration of land and environmental values to a surface mine site after the coal is extracted. Reclamation operations are usually underway as soon as the coal has been removed from a mine site. The process includes restoring the land to its approximate original appearance by restoring topsoil and planting native grasses and ground covers.

Recovery - The proportion or percentage of coal or ore mined from the original seam or deposit.

Red dog - A nonvolatile combustion product of the oxidation of coal or coal refuse. Most commonly applied to material resulting from in situ, uncontrolled burning of coal or coal refuse piles. It is similar to coal ash.

Regulator - Device (wall, door) used to control the volume of air in an air split.

Reserve – That portion of the identified coal resource that can be economically mined at the time of determination. The reserve is derived by applying a recovery factor to that component of the identified coal resource designated as the reserve base.

Resin bolting - A method of permanent roof support in which steel rods are grouted with resin.

Resources – Concentrations of coal in such forms that economic extraction is currently or may become feasible. Coal resources broken down by identified and undiscovered resources. Identified coal resources are classified as demonstrated and inferred. Demonstrated resources are further broken down as measured and indicated. Undiscovered resources are broken down as hypothetical and speculative.

Respirable dust - Dust particles 5 microns or less in size.

Respirable dust sample - A sample collected with an approved coal mine dust sampler unit attached to a miner, or so positioned as to measure the concentration of respirable dust to which the miner is exposed, and operated continuously over an entire work shift of such miner.

Retreat mining - A system of robbing pillars in which the robbing line, or line through the faces of the pillars being extracted, retreats from the boundary toward the shaft or mine mouth.

Return - The air or ventilation that has passed through all the working faces of a split.

Return idler - The idler or roller underneath the cover or cover plates on which the conveyor belt rides after the load which it was carrying has been dumped at the head section and starts the return trip toward the foot section.

Rib - The side of a pillar or the wall of an entry. The solid coal on the side of any underground passage. Same as rib pillar.

Rider - A thin seam of coal overlying a thicker one.

Ripper - A coal extraction machine that works by tearing the coal from the face.

Rob - To extract pillars of coal previously left for support.

Robbed out area - Describes that part of a mine from which the pillars have been removed.

Roll - (1) A high place in the bottom or a low place in the top of a mine passage, (2) a local thickening of roof or floor strata, causing thinning of a coal seam.

Roll protection - A framework, safety canopy, or similar protection for the operator when equipment overturns.

Roof - The stratum of rock or other material above a coal seam; the overhead surface of a coal working place. Same as "back" or "top."

Roof bolt - A long steel bolt driven into the roof of underground excavations to support the roof, preventing and limiting the extent of roof falls. The unit consists of the bolt (up to 4 feet long), steel plate, expansion shell, and pal nut. The use of roof bolts eliminates the need for timbering by fastening together, or "laminating," several weaker layers of roof strata to build a "beam."

Roof fall - A coal mine cave-in especially in permanent areas such as entries.

Roof jack - A screw- or pump-type hydraulic extension post made of steel and used as temporary roof support.

Roof sag - The sinking, bending, or curving of the roof, especially in the middle, from weight or pressure.

Roof stress - Unbalanced internal forces in the roof or sides, created when coal is extracted.

Roof support – Posts, jacks, roof bolts and beams used to support the rock overlying a coal seam in an underground mine. A good roof support plan is part of mine safety and coal extraction.

Roof trusses - A combination of steel rods anchored into the roof to create zones of compression and tension forces and provide better support for weak roof and roof over wide areas.

Room and pillar mining – A method of underground mining in which approximately half of the coal is left in place to support the roof of the active mining area. Large "pillars" are left while "rooms" of coal are extracted.

Room neck - The short passage from the entry into a room.

Round - Planned pattern of drill holes fired in sequence in tunneling, shaft sinking, or stopping. First the cut holes are fired, followed by relief, lifter, and rib holes.

Royalty - The payment of a certain stipulated sum on the mineral produced.

Rubbing surface - The total area (top, bottom, and sides) of an airway.

Run-of-mine - Raw material as it exists in the mine; average grade or quality.

Safety fuse - A train of powder enclosed in cotton, jute yarn, or waterproofing compounds, which burns at a uniform rate; used for firing a cap containing the detonation compound which in turn sets off the explosive charge.

Safety lamp - A lamp with steel wire gauze covering every opening from the inside to the outside so as to prevent the passage of flame should explosive gas be encountered.

Sampling - Cutting a representative part of an ore (or coal) deposit, which should truly represent its average value.

Sandstone - A sedimentary rock consisting of quartz sand united by some cementing material, such as iron oxide or calcium carbonate.

Scaling - Removal of loose rock from the roof or walls. This work is dangerous and a long bar (called a scaling bar) is often used.

Scoop - A rubber tired-, battery- or diesel-powered piece of equipment designed for cleaning runways and hauling supplies.

Scrubber – Any of several forms of chemical/physical devices that remove sulfur compounds formed during coal combustion. These devices, technically known as flue gas desulfurization systems, combine the sulfur in gaseous emissions with another chemical medium to form inert "sludge," which must then be removed for disposal.

Seam - A stratum or bed of coal.

Secondary roof - The roof strata immediately above the coalbed, requiring support during the excavating of coal.

Section - A portion of the working area of a mine.

Selective mining - The object of selective mining is to obtain a relatively high-grade mine product; this usually entails the use of a much more expensive stopping system and high exploration and development costs in searching for and developing the separate bunches, stringers, lenses, and bands of ore.

Self-contained breathing apparatus - A self-contained supply of oxygen used during rescue work from coal mine fires and explosions; same as SCSR (self-contained self-rescuer).

Self-rescuer – A small filtering device carried by a coal miner underground, either on his belt or in his pocket, to provide him with immediate protection against carbon monoxide and smoke in case of a mine fire or explosion. It is a small canister with a mouthpiece directly attached to it. The wearer breathes through the mouth, the nose being closed by a clip. The canister contains a layer of fused calcium chloride that absorbs water vapor from the mine air. The device is used for escape purposes only because it does not sustain life in atmospheres containing deficient oxygen. The length of time a self-rescuer can be used is governed mainly by the humidity in the mine air, usually between 30 minutes and one hour.

Severance – The separation of a mineral interest from other interests in the land by grant or reservation. A mineral dead or grant of the land reserving a mineral interest, by the landowner before leasing, accomplishes a severance as does his execution of a mineral lease.

Shaft - A primary vertical or non-vertical opening through mine strata used for ventilation or drainage and/or for hoisting of personnel or materials; connects the surface with underground workings.

Shaft mine – An underground mine in which the main entry or access is by means of a vertical shaft.

Shale - A rock formed by consolidation of clay, mud, or silt, having a laminated structure and composed of minerals essentially unaltered since deposition.

Shearer - A mining machine for longwall faces that uses a rotating action to "shear" the material from the face as it progresses along the face.

Shift - The number of hours or the part of any day worked.

Shortwall – An underground mining method in which small areas are worked (15 to 150 feet) by a continuous miner in conjunction with the use of hydraulic roof supports.

Shuttle car – A self-discharging truck, generally with rubber tires or caterpillar-type treads, used for receiving coal from the loading or mining machine and transferring it to an underground loading point, mine railway or belt conveyor system.

Sinking - The process by which a shaft is driven.

Skid - A track-mounted vehicle used to hold trips or cars from running out of control. Also it is a flat-bottom personnel or equipment carrier used in low coal.

Skip - A car being hoisted from a slope or shaft.

Slack - Small coal; the finest-sized soft coal, usually less than one inch in diameter.

Slag - The waste product of the process of smelting.

Slate - A miner's term for any shale or slate accompanying coal. Geologically, it is a dense, fine-textured, metamorphic rock, which has excellent parallel cleavage so that it breaks into thin plates or pencil-like shapes.

Slate bar - The proper long-handled tool used to pry down loose and hazardous material from roof, face, and ribs.

Slickenside - A smooth, striated, polished surface produced on rock by friction.

Slip - A fault. A smooth joint or crack where the strata have moved on each other.

Slope - Primary inclined opening, connection the surface with the underground workings.

Slope mine – An underground mine with an opening that slopes upward or downward to the coal seam.

Sloughing - The slow crumbling and falling away of material from roof, rib, and face.

Solid - Mineral that has not been undermined, sheared out, or otherwise prepared for blasting.

Sounding - Knocking on a roof to see whether it is sound and safe to work under.

Spad – A spad is a flat spike hammered into a wooden plug anchored in a hole drilled into the mine ceiling from which is threaded a plumb line. The spad is an underground survey station similar to the use of stakes in marking survey points on the surface. A pointer spad, or sight spad, is a station that allows a mine foreman to visually align entries or breaks from the main spad.

Span - The horizontal distance between the side supports or solid abutments along sides of a roadway.

Specific gravity - The weight of a substance compared with the weight of an equal volume of pure water at 4 degrees Celsius.

Split - Any division or branch of the ventilating current. Also, the workings ventilated by one branch. Also, to divide a pillar by driving one or more roads through it.

Squeeze - The settling, without breaking, of the roof and the gradual upheaval of the floor of a mine due to the weight of the overlying strata.

Steeply inclined - Said of deposits and coal seams with a dip of from 0.7 to 1 rad (40 degrees to 60 degrees).

Stemming - The noncombustible material used on top or in front of a charge or explosive.

Strike - The direction of the line of intersection of a bed or vein with the horizontal plane. The strike of a bed is the direction of a straight line that connects two points of equal elevation on the bed.

Stripping ratio – The unit amount of overburden that must be removed to gain access to a similar unit amount of coal or mineral material.

Stump - Any small pillar.

Subbituminous – Coal of a rank intermediate between lignite and bituminous.

Subsidence – The gradual sinking, or sometimes abrupt collapse, of the rock and soil layers into an underground mine. Structures and surface features above the subsidence area can be affected.

Sump - The bottom of a shaft, or any other place in a mine, that is used as a collecting point for drainage water.

Sumping - To force the cutter bar of a machine into or under the coal. Also called a sumping cut, or sumping in.

Support - The all-important function of keeping the mine workings open. As a verb, it refers to this function; as a noun it refers to all the equipment and materials—timber, roof bolts, concrete, steel, etc.—that are used to carry out this function.

Surface mine – A mine in which the coal lies near the surface and can be extracted by removing the covering layers of rock and soil.

Suspension - Weaker strata hanging from stronger, overlying strata by means of roof bolts.

Syncline - A fold in rock in which the strata dip inward from both sides toward the axis. The opposite of anticline.

Tailgate - A subsidiary gate road to a conveyor face as opposed to a main gate. The tailgate commonly acts as the return airway and supplies road to the face.

Tailpiece - Also known as foot section pulley. The pulley or roller in the tail or foot section of a belt conveyor around which the belt runs.

Tail section - A term used in both belt and chain conveyor work to designate that portion of the conveyor at the extreme opposite end from the delivery point. In either type of conveyor it consists of a frame and either a sprocket or a drum on which the chain or belt travels, plus such other devices as may be required for adjusting belt or chain tension.

Tension - The act of stretching.

Tertiary - Lateral or panel openings (e.g., ramp, crosscut).

Through-steel - A system of dust collection from rock or roof drilling. The drill steel is hollow, and a vacuum is applied at the base, pulling the dust through the steel and into a receptacle on the machine.

Timber - A collective term for underground wooden supports.

Timbering - The setting of timber supports in mine workings or shafts for protection against falls from roof, face, or rib.

Timber set - A timber frame to support the roof, sides, and sometimes the floor of mine roadways or shafts.

Tipple - Originally the place where the mine cars were tipped and emptied of their coal, and still used in that same sense, although now more generally applied to the surface structures of a mine, including the preparation plant and loading tracks.

Ton – A short or net ton is equal to 2,000 pounds; a long or British ton is 2,240 pounds; a metric ton is approximately 2,205 pounds.

Top - A mine roof; same as "back."

Torque wrench - A wrench that indicates, as on a dial, the amount of torque (in units of foot-pounds) exerted in tightening a roof bolt.

Tractor - A battery-operated piece of equipment that pulls trailers, skids, or personnel carriers. Also used for supplies.

Tram - Used in connection with moving self-propelled mining equipment. A tramming motor may refer to an electric locomotive used for hauling loaded trips or it may refer to the motor in a cutting machine that supplies the power for moving or tramming the machine.

Transfer - A vertical or inclined connection between two or more levels and used as an ore pass.

Transfer point - Location in the materials handling system, either haulage or hoisting, where bulk material is transferred between conveyances.

Trip - A train of mine cars.

Troughing idlers - The idlers, located on the upper framework of a belt conveyor, which support the loaded belt. They are so mounted that the loaded belt forms a trough in the direction of travel, which reduces spillage and increases the carrying capacity of a belt for a given width.

Tunnel - A horizontal, or near-horizontal, underground passage, entry, or haulageway, that is open to the surface at both ends. A tunnel (as opposed to an adit) must pass completely through a hill or mountain.

Ultimate analysis - Precise determination, by chemical means, of the elements and compounds in coal.

Undercut - To cut below or undermine the coal face by chipping away the coal by pick or mining machine. In some localities the terms "undermine" or "underhole" are used.

Underground mine – Also known as a "deep" mine. Usually located several hundred feet below the earth's surface, an underground mine's coal is removed mechanically and transferred by shuttle car or conveyor to the surface.

Underground station - An enlargement of an entry, drift, or level at a shaft at which cages stop to receive and discharge cars, personnel, and material. An underground station is any location where stationary electrical equipment is installed. This includes pump rooms, compressor rooms, hoist rooms, battery-charging rooms, etc.

Unit train – A long train of between 60 and 150 or more hopper cars, carrying only coal between a single mine and destination.

Universal coal cutter - A type of coal cutting machine which is designed to make horizontal cuts in a coal face at any point between the bottom and top or to make shearing cuts at any point between the two ribs of the place. The cutter bar can be twisted to make cuts at any angle to the horizontal or vertical.

Upcast shaft - A shaft through which air leaves the mine.

Valuation - The act or process of valuing or of estimating the value or worth; appraisal.

Velocity - Rate of airflow in lineal feet per minute.

Ventilation - The provision of a directed flow of fresh and return air along all underground roadways, traveling roads, workings, and service parts.

Violation - The breaking of any state or federal mining law.

Virgin - Unworked; untouched; often said of areas where there has been no coal mining.

Void - A general term for pore space or other reopenings in rock. In addition to pore space, the term includes vesicles, solution cavities, or any openings either primary or secondary.

Volatile matter - The gaseous part, mostly hydrocarbons, of coal.

W

Waste - That rock or mineral which must be removed from a mine to keep the mining scheme practical, but which has no value.

Water Gauge (standard U-tube) - Instrument that measures differential pressures in inches of water.

Wedge - A piece of wood tapering to a thin edge and used for tightening in conventional timbering.

Weight - Fracturing and lowering of the roof strata at the face as a result of mining operations, as in "taking weight".

White damp - Carbon monoxide, CO. A gas that may be present in the afterdamp of a gas- or coal-dust explosion, or in the gases given off by a mine fire; also one of the constituents of the gases produced by blasting. Rarely found in mines under other circumstances. It is absorbed by the hemoglobin of the blood to the exclusion of oxygen. One-tenth of 1% (.001) may be fatal in 10 minutes.

Width - The thickness of a lode measured at right angles to the dip.

Winning - The excavation, loading, and removal of coal or ore from the ground; winning follows development.

Winze - Secondary or tertiary vertical or near-vertical opening sunk from a point inside a mine for the purpose of connecting with a lower level or of exploring the ground for a limited depth below a level.

Wire rope - A steel wire rope used for winding in shafts and underground haulages. Wire ropes are made from medium carbon steels. Various constructions of wire rope are designated by the number of strands in the rope and the number of wires in each strand. The following are some common terms encountered:

airplane strand; cablelaid rope; cane rope; elevator rope; extra-flexible hoisting rope; flat rope; flattened-strand rope; guy rope; guy strand; hand rope; haulage rope; hawser; hoisting rope; lang lay rope; lay; left lay rope; left twist; nonspinning rope; regular lay; reverse-laid rope; rheostat rope; right lay; right twist; running rope; special flexible hoisting rope; standing rope; towing hawser; transmission rope.

Working - When a coal seam is being squeezed by pressure from roof and floor, it emits creaking noises and is said to be "working". This often serves as a warning to the miners that additional support is needed.

Working face - Any place in a mine where material is extracted during a mining cycle.

Working place - From the outby side of the last open crosscut to the face.

Workings - The entire system of openings in a mine for the purpose of exploitation.

Working section - From the faces to the point where coal is loaded onto belts or rail cars to begin its trip to the outside.

About the Authors

Thurman I. Miller, approaching the age of 96 as of this writing, is the author of four previous books including *Earned in Blood: My Journey from Old-Breed Marine to the Most Dangerous Job in America*, published by St. Martin's Press. He served as Gunny Sergeant in the First Marine Division during World War II, fighting in the South Pacific, and left the service in 1945 qualified as a First Sergeant. He retired from the coal mine in 1980 after a career spanning nearly four decades. He currently lives near Beckley, West Virginia.

David T. Miller is Thurman's youngest son and has edited and contributed to more than a dozen books. This is his fifth collaboration with his father. He is based in Lexington, Kentucky.

Illustrations

Note: We have endeavored to use personally-owned or public domain materials wherever possible. In the case of donated materials we have tried to determine their source, although given the time period covered in this book that's not always possible. If you are aware of any credit omissions please contact the authors and we will make sure they are appropriately credited in a future edition.Panoramic photos used here, on DVD, or on the author's website are believed to be the work of Rufus E. "Red" Ribble although are not copyrighted. Many of these photos are still available as prints from George and Melody Bragg at GEM Publications in Beaver, WV.

Page	Source
Cover	Reversed/cropped detail from Miners coming home from morning shift Mullens Smokeless Coal Company, Mullens Mine, Harmco, Wyoming County, WV, National Archives and Records Administration (NARA) 540933. Harmco is now a part of Mullens, on the west side.
x-xiv	Collection of the author. The author thanks John Lewis for the gift of the underground mine maps.
1	Harry Fain, coal loader, removes "bug dust" from undercut made by cutting machine. NARA 541484
2	Collection of the author
3	West Virginia Division of Tourism (reversed and cropped)
4	Milong Bond, tipple worker, taking a bath. There is no washhouse for mine nor tipple workers. Mullens Smokeless Coal Company, Mullens Mine, Harmco, Wyoming County, West Virginia. NARA 540957
6	Typical houses and street. Comment of miner, The mine is about worked out and the houses are sure worked out. NARA 540954
7	Scott's Run, West Virginia. Pursglove Mines Nos. 3 and 4 - This is the largest company of Scott's Run. NARA - 518378
8	Tipple. P V & K Coal Company, Clover Gap Mine, Lejunior, Harlan County, Kentucky. NARA 541398
9	Collection of the author
10	Group of breaker boys. Smallest is Sam Belloma. Pittston, Pa. NARA 523383.
11	Coal breaker boys, circa 1910. Library of Congress LC-DIG-det-4a16385. British child miner photographer unknown.
13	Dr. R. V. Tokar, company doctor, making house call. This house in privately owned and is built on company-owned land which was leased for 99 years. U.S. Coal and Coke Company, Gary Mines,

	Gary, McDowell County, West Virginia. NARA 540857
14	Recie Marshall Miller, collection of the author.
21	Courtesy Coal India Limited
22	Collection of the author
23	Harry Fain, coal loader, places and secures safety timber close to the face where he will work. Inland Steel Company. NARA 541487
24	Collection of the author
25	Courtesy Arch Coal
26	Collection of the author
28	Collection of the author
31	Adapted by the editor from original patent document for Joy cutting machine controller. Public domain.
33	Coal products tree courtesy Beckley Exhibition Coal Mine
34	Courtesy Kentucky Geological Survey, University of Kentucky
35	Photo by Lewis Hine, Scott's Run, West Virginia. (Woman gathering coal.) NARA 518407
36	Collection of the author
37	Tipple, PV&K Coal Company, Harlan County, Kentucky. NARA 541398.
38	Martin County home, Wikimedia Commons
39	Courtesy coalcampusa.com
41	Collection of the author
43	Adapted from Lessons In Electric Circuits copyright (c) 2000-2015 Tony R. Kuphaldt. Used under the terms of the Design Science License
45	Courtesy Jeffrey Manufacturing Company
47	Courtesy Joy Manufacturing Company
49	Wikimedia Commons, used under Creative Commons Attribution 2.0 Generic license, https://commons.wikimedia.org/wiki/File:Mine equipment Exhibition Coal Mine Beckley WV 8545
51	Collection of the author
52	Coal Mine Man Trip courtesy Coal Association of Canada
54	Courtesy Koppers Coal Company and coalcampusa.com
57	Interior of bathhouse for miners. Debardeleben Coal Corporation, Sipsey Mine, Sipsey, Walker County, Alabama. NARA 540645
58	Electricity Wheel, courtesy Coyne Electrical School, Chicago, IL
60	Adapted from Lessons In Electric Circuits copyright (c) 2000-2015 Tony R. Kuphaldt. Used under the terms of the Design Science License
63	Lunchbox collection of the author
70	Map detail collection of the author
74	Locomotive image courtesy National Park Service
76	Pay stub collection of the author

79	Courtesy the Cardox Corporation
81	Blasting with airdox, Western Monarch Mine, East Coulee, courtesy Provincial Archives of Alberta, Canada
84	Chicago postcard courtesy https://chuckmanchicagonostalgia.wordpress.com /2010/12/16/postcard-chicago-state-street-aerial-flags-of-different-countries-cars-buses-signs-late-1950s/
87	Back Cover Amazing Stories volume 1, No. 1, courtesy Coyne Electrical School
88	Training certificate collection of the author
94	Adapted from Lessons In Electric Circuits copyright (c) 2000-2015 Tony R. Kuphaldt. Used under the terms of the Design Science License
96	Adapted from Lessons In Electric Circuits copyright (c) 2000-2015 Tony R. Kuphaldt. Used under the terms of the Design Science License
99	Courtesy Earl Dotter, www.earldotter.com
103	Miners boarding cars of man trip just before going underground. Koppers Coal Division, Kopperston. NARA 540929
109	Harold Fickes, motorman, shuttling car load of mine props. Chicago, Wilmington & Franklin Coal Company, New Orient. NARA 540342
111	Library of Congress Prints and Photographs Division Washington, D.C. 20540 USA, Wikimedia Commons Jlewis-cph3c20320.jpg
112	"Clear the Tracks for War Shipments. Buy Coal Now" NARA 513507
113	NARA, http://media.nara.gov/legislative/clifford-berryman/7-19-1922_V-090_46_Berryman.jpg
115	Courtesy http://www.presidency.ucsb.edu/
116	Berryman, NARA 5730852
120	The New York Times, October 4, 1915
121	Collection of the author
122	The Fairmont West Virginian, pg. 1, December 9, 1907
124	Sandia National Laboratories, May 29, 2007, "Sandia research indicates that lightning was the likely cause of Sago Mine explosion," https://share.sandia.gov/news/resources/ releases/2007/sago.html
126	Hard hat, collection of the author
129	Martin County home, Wikimedia Commons
130	Collection of the author
134	Saturday afternoon street scene. Welch, McDowell County, West Virginia. NARA 541004
135	Welch, Wikimedia Commons
138	Collection of the author
133	Miners and mules, circa 1908. Public domain.

141	Courtesy www.wvencyclopedia.org
144	Raleigh Register, Beckley, WV, August 3, 1997
146	Courtesy Saturday Evening Post, Feb. 6, 1960

Afterword

In both my Marine and mining careers I watched for what I could learn—the unusual, eyes aware of the danger. As I bound up the wounds of some of my marine comrades, so I bound up the wounds of many coal miner friends when they got a minor injury. And so I bound up my own wounds, physical and psychic. I hope whomever reads this will come away with a different view of the daily life of the working man, the coal miner, the electrician, the mechanic.

As I finish this story of my mining career, and I hope, the story of "the coal miner" in general, I arrive at this point in my life as the very last of our very large family. My brothers and sisters, nieces and nephews, indeed my large circle of friends—all gone, as I approach my 96th birthday. I have no complaint, however; my three wonderful children have given me six grandchildren, six great-grandchildren and three great-great grandchildren. And so after five years and three weeks of service in the Marine Corps, years so many friends did not survive, and thirty-five years a coal miner, which again claimed so many friends, I count myself fortunate. I thank the Lord; how Great thou art.

My late wife Recie occasionally wrote poetry, though she rarely shared it with anyone. The life of a miner (or his wife, sister or daughter) was a main theme, and below are two of her poems. I will give her the last word.

Homecoming

Back home at last to peace and joy
To a job you could enjoy
The service to your country a thing of the past
Job hunting you went, with hope and joy, and
I was thinking how happy I would be
To have a husband home on time at last
But jobs were scarce.

Each day you came home in despair
The thing I dreaded most was here at last
The cold, dark mine would be your future
I walked, I prayed each day for your safe return
The camp we lived in was as friendly as could be
But each day if we heard an ambulance
We would gather and wonder
Which one would it be?
With your dark faces/It was difficult to see.
Is it my Dad, or my husband,
free at last from that cold, dark hole?

The life of a miner.
Through hours of toil and labor, the miners they do slave
Each day and hour their life they give
As enjoyment they do crave
While in the mines they load the coal
Their backs nearly break
They work for food and clothing
For their dear children's sake
Their life shortens hour by hour
The days go slowly by
They pray to God to give them rest;
And die without a sigh

Addenda

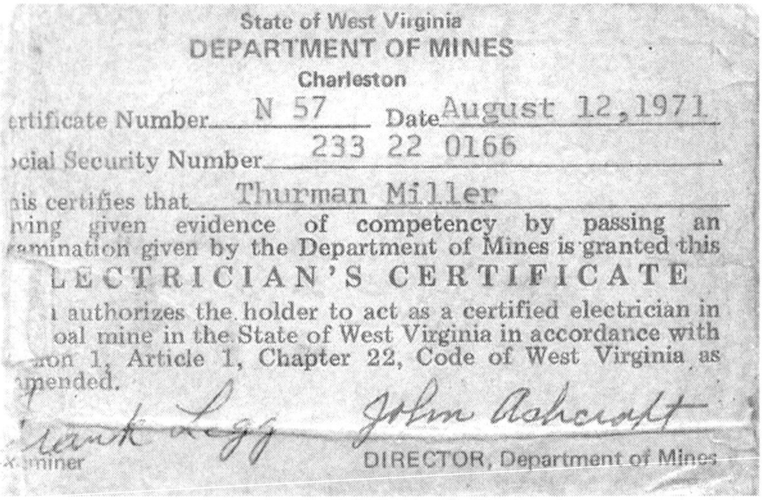

State of West Virginia
DEPARTMENT OF MINES
Charleston

Certificate Number __N 57__ Date __August 12, 1971__

Social Security Number __233 22 0166__

This certifies that __Thurman Miller__ having given evidence of competency by passing an examination given by the Department of Mines is granted this

ELECTRICIAN'S CERTIFICATE

This authorizes the holder to act as a certified electrician in a coal mine in the State of West Virginia in accordance with Section 1, Article 1, Chapter 22, Code of West Virginia as amended.

Examiner

DIRECTOR, Department of Mines

UNITED STATES
DEPARTMENT OF THE INTERIOR
BUREAU OF MINES
233-22-0166
THURMAN I MILLER
QUALIFIED FOR SURFACE   EXP
ELECTRICAL (SURFACE)   08/75

Be sure to write your name PLAINLY. THIS PART OF THIS SHEET WILL BE RETURNED TO YOU WITH YOUR DEPARTMENT GRADE. A passing grade is 75%. 75% to 79% is considered satisfactory; 80% to 84% good; 85% to 89% very good; 90% to 94% excellent; 95% to 100% superior.

NAME *Thurman Miller* DEPARTMENT *Direct Curre...*

STUDENT NUMBER 53-FE-291 DATE 6/19/53 GRADE 93

Test No - C5 INSTRUCTOR'S SIGNATURE *Paul L. Fries*

Be sure to write your name PLAINLY. THIS PART OF THIS SHEET WILL BE RETURNED TO YOU WITH YOUR DEPARTMENT GRADE. A passing grade is 75%. 75% to 79% is considered satisfactory; 80% to 84% good; 85% to 89% very good; 90% to 94% excellent; 95% to 100% superior.

NAME MILLER, T.I. DEPARTMENT BE+C

STUDENT NUMBER 53-FE-291 DATE 5/8/53 GRADE 97

B2 INSTRUCTOR'S SIGNATURE *S.T. Cherry*

Be sure to write your name PLAINLY. THIS PART OF THIS SHEET WILL BE RETURNED TO YOU WITH YOUR DEPARTMENT GRADE. A passing grade is 75%. 75% to 79% is considered satisfactory; 80% to 84% good; 85% to 89% very good; 90% to 94% excellent; 95% to 100% superior.

NAME *Thurman Miller* DEPARTMENT W & R

STUDENT NUMBER 53/FE/291 DATE 5/24/53 GRADE 93

B2 (test 20) INSTRUCTOR'S SIGNATURE *S S Harrelson*

188

G-11

COYNE ELECTRICAL AND TELEVISION-RADIO SCHOOL
500 SOUTH PAULINA STREET   •   CHICAGO 12, ILLINOIS

OFFICIAL TRANSCRIPT OF RECORD

Graduate's Name __Thurman Miller__   Town __Otsego,__

Address _____ State __Virginia__

Course Enrolled for __Day Electrical (15 weeks.)__

Date Started __4-20-53__ Date Left School __Int. - 7-20-53.__   Graduated: ☐ Yes ☒ No

SUMMARY OF GRADES

Dept.	Basic Elec. & Circuits I	Basic Elec. & Circuits II	Wiring and Repair I	Direct Current I	Alternating Current I	Industrial Electronics I	Wiring and Repair II	Direct Current II	Alternating Current II	Industrial Electronics II	Electric Refrig. I	Average Grade
Grade	97		93	94								
Dept.	Basic Radio I	Basic Radio II	Radio Const. & Rep. I	Radio Const. & Rep. II	Radio Service I	T.V. & F.M. Circuits I	Television Service I	Radio Service II	T.V. & F.M. Circuits II	Television Service II	Electric Refrig. II	
Grade												

Shop Work: __Very good__   Theory: __Very good__

Industry: __Very good__   Co-operation: __Very good__

Comments: _____

.WV Mine Disasters 1884 to 2010

DATE	COMPANY	MINE	LOCATION	NATURE OF ACCIDENT	VICTIMS
JAN. 21, 1886	ORREL COAL COMPANY	MT. BROOK	NEWBURG	EXPLOSION	39
NOV. 20, 1894	BLANCH COAL CO.	BLANCH	STANDARD	EXPLOSION	8
MAR. 06, 1900	RED ASH COAL COMPANY	RED ASH	RED ASH	EXPLOSION	46
NOV. 02, 1900	SOUTHERN COAL & TRANSPORTATION CO.	BERRYBURG	BERRYBURG	POWDER EXPLO.	15
MAY 15, 1901	GEORGE'S CREEK COAL & IRON CO.	CHATHAM	FARMINGTON	EXPLOSION	10
SEP. 15, 1902	ALGOMA COAL AND COKE	ALGOMA NO. 7	ALGOMA	EXPLOSION	17
SEP. 22, 1902	NEW CENTRAL COAL CO.	STAFFORD	STAFFORD	EXPLOSION	6
FEB. 26, 1905	GRAPEVINE COAL CO.	GRAPEVINE	WILCOE	EXPLOSION	7
MAR. 19, 1905	NEW RIVER SMOKELESS COAL CO.	RUSHRUN/REDASH	RED ASH	EXPLOSION	24
APR. 20, 1905	CABIN CREEK MINING CO.	CABIN CREEK	KAYFORD	POWDER EXPLO.	6
JUL. 05, 1905	TIDEWATER COAL & COKE CO.	TIDEWATER	VIVIAN	EXPLOSION	5
NOV. 04, 1905	TIDEWATER COAL & COKE CO.	TIDEWATER	VIVIAN	EXPLOSION	7
DEC. 04, 1905	CARDIFF COAL CO.	HORTON	CABIN CREEK	MINE FIRE	7
JAN. 04, 1906	COALDALE COAL & COKE CO.	COALDALE	COALDALE	EXPLOSION	22
JAN. 18, 1906	DETROIT & KANAWHA COAL CO.	DETROIT	PAINT CREEK	EXPLOSION	18
FEB. 08, 1906	STUART COLLIERY CO.	PARRAL	PARRAL	EXPLOSION	23
MAR. 22, 1906	CENTURY COAL CO.	CENTURY	CENTURY	EXPLOSION	23
DEC. 14, 1906	PULASKI IRON CO.	PULASKI	ECKMAN	POWDER EXPLO.	6*
JAN. 26, 1907	LORENTZ	LORENTZ	PENCO	POWDER EXPLO.	12
JAN. 29, 1907	STUART COLLIERY CO.	STUART	STUART	EXPLOSION	85
FEB. 04, 1907	DAVIS COAL & COKE CO.	THOMAS	THOMAS	EXPLOSION	25
MAY 01, 1907	WHITE OAK FUEL CO.	WHIPPLE	SCARBRO	EXPLOSION	46
DEC. 06, 1907	FAIRMONT COAL CO.	MONONGAH 6 & 8	MONONGAH	EXPLOSION	361
JAN. 30, 1908	NEW RIVER VALLEY COAL CO.	BACKMAN	HAWKS NEST	EXPLOSION	9
DEC. 29, 1908	POCAHONTAS COLLERIES CO.	LICK BRANCH	SWITCHBACK	EXPLOSION	50
JAN. 12, 1909	POCAHONTAS COLLERIES CO.	LICK BRANCH	SWITCHBACK	EXPLOSION	67
MAR. 31, 1909	BEURY BROTHERS COAL CO.	ECHO	BEURY	DYNAMITE EXPLO.	16
DEC. 31, 1910	RED JACKET CONS. COAL & COKE CO.	LICK FORK	THACKER	HAULAGE	10
APR. 24, 1911	DAVIS COAL & COKE CO.	OTT NO. 20	ELK GARDEN	EXPLOSION	23

AUG. 01, 1911	STANDARD POCAHONTAS FUEL CO.	STANDARD	CAPLES	EXPLOSION	6
NOV. 18, 1911	BOTTOM CREEK COAL & COKE CO.	BOTTOM CREEK	VIVIAN	EXPLOSION	18
MAR. 26, 1912	JED COAL AND COKE CO.	JED	JED	EXPLOSION	80
JULY 11, 1912	BEN FRANKLIN COAL CO.	PANAMA	MOUNDSVILLE	EXPLOSION	8
APR. 28, 1914	NEW RIVER COLLIERIES CO., THE	ECCLES NO. 5 & 6	ECCLES	EXPLOSION	183
JUNE 30, 1914	SYCAMORE COAL CO.	CINDERELLA	CINDERELLA	SUFFOCATION	5
FEB. 6, 1915	NEW RIVER CO.	CARLISLE	CARLISLE	EXPLOSION	22
MAR. 2, 1915	NEW RIVER & POCAHONTAS CONSOL. CO.	LAYLAND NO. 3	LAYLAND	EXPLOSION	112
MAR. 30, 1915	HANNA COAL CO.	BOOMER NO. 2	BOOMER	EXPLOSION	23
MAR. 28, 1916	KING COAL CO.	KING NO. 28	VIVIAN	EXPLOSION	10
OCT. 19, 1916	JAMISON COAL AND COKE CO.	JAMISON NO. 7	BARRACKVILLE	EXPLOSION	10
APR. 18, 1917	HUTCHINSON COAL CO.	LYNDEN	MASON	EXPLOSION	5
DEC. 15, 1917	YUKON POCAHONTAS COAL CO.	YUKON NO. 1	SUSANNA	EXPLOSION	18
MAY 20, 1918	MILL CREEK CANNEL MINING CO.	VILLA	CHARLESTON	MINE FIRE	13
JULY 18, 1919	HOUSTON COLLIERIES CO.	CARSWELL	KIMBALL	EXPLOSION	7
AUG. 6, 1919	NEW RIVER AND POCAHONTAS CONSOLIDATED	WEIRWOOD	WEIRWOOD	EXPLOSION	7
MAY 22, 1920	MALLORY COAL CO.	MALLORY NO. 3	MALLORY	ROOF FALL	5
SEPT.23, 1922	RALEIGH-WYOMING COAL CO.	GLEN ROGERS #2	GLENROGERS	FALLING CAGE	5
MAR. 2, 1923	WEYANOKE COAL & COKE CO.	ARISTA	ARISTA	EXPLOSION	10
NOV. 06, 1923	RALEIGH-WYOMING COAL CO.	GLEN ROGERS	BECKLEY	EXPLOSION	27
MAR. 28, 1924	YUKON POCAHONTAS COAL CO.	YUKON NO. 2	YUKON	EXPLOSION	24
APR. 28, 1924	WHEELING STEEL CORP.	BENWOOD	BENWOOD	EXPLOSION	119
MAR. 17, 1925	BETHLEHEM MINES CORP.	BARRACKSVILLE	BARRACKSVILLE	EXPLOSION	33
JAN. 14, 1926	JAMISON COAL & COKE CO.	JAMISON NO. 8	FARMINGTON	EXPLOSION	19
MAR. 8, 1926	CRAB ORCHARD IMPROVEMENT CO.	ECCLES NO. 5	ECCLES	EXPLOSION	19
NOV. 15, 1926	GLENDALE GAS COAL CO.	MOUND SHAFT	MOUNDSVILLE	EXPLOSION	5
APR. 30, 1927	NEW ENGLAND FUEL & TRANS. CO.	FEDERAL NO. 3	EVERTTVILLE	EXPLOSION	97
MAY 13, 1927	CENTRAL POCAHONTAS COAL CO.	SHANNON BR. 3	CAPELS	EXPLOSION	8
APR. 2, 1928	KEYSTONE COAL AND COKE CO.	KEYSTONE NO. 2	KEYSTONE	EXPLOSION	8
MAY 22, 1928	YUKON POCAHONTAS COAL CO.	YUKON NO. 1	YUKON	EXPLOSION	17
JUNE 20, 1928	NATIONAL FUEL CO.	NO. 1	NATIONAL	EXPLOSION	7

OCT. 22, 1928	MACALPIN COAL CO.	MCALPIN	MCALPIN	EXPLOSION	6
NOV. 30, 1928	PRINCESS POCAHONTAS COAL CORP.	PRINCESS POCAHONTAS	RODERFIELD	EXPLOSION	6
JAN. 26, 1929	KINGSTON POCAHONTAS COAL CO. INC.	KINGSTON NO. 5	KINGSTON	EXPLOSION	14
JAN. 19, 1930	LILLYBROOK COAL CO.	NO. 1	LILLYBROOK	EXPLOSION	8
MAR. 26, 1930	CROWN COAL CO.	YUKON	ARNETTSVILLE	EXPLOSION	12
JAN. 6, 1931	RALEIGH-WYOMING COAL CO.	GLEN ROGERS #2	GLEN ROGERS	EXPLOSION	8
NOV. 3, 1931	ISLAND CREEK COAL CO.	NO. 20	WHITMAN	EXPLOSION	5
MAY 12, 1935	BETHLEHEM MINES CORP.	NO. 41	BARRACKVILLE	FIRE IN SHAFT	6
SEPT. 2, 1936	HUTCHINSON COAL CO.	MACBETH	MACBETH	EXPLOSION	10
MAR. 11, 1937	HUTCHINSON COAL CO.	MACBETH	MACBETH	EXPLOSION	18
JAN. 10, 1940	POND CREEK POCAHONTAS COAL CO.	NO. 1	BARTLEY	EXPLOSION	91
DEC. 17, 1940	RALEIGH COAL & COKE CO.	NO. 4	RALEIGH	EXPLOSION	9
JAN. 22, 1941	KOPPERS COAL CO.	CARSWELL	CARSWELL	EXPLOSION	6
MAY 12, 1942	CHRISTOPHER COAL CO.	CHRISTOPHER NO. 3	OSAGE	EXPLOSION	56
MAY 18, 1942	HITCHMAN COAL & COKE CO.	HITCHMAN	BENWOOD	EXPLOSION	5
JULY 9, 1942	PURSGLOVE COAL MINING CO.	PURSGLOVE NO. 2	PURSGLOVE	EXPLOSION	20
DEC. 15, 1942	WYATT COAL CO.	LAING NO. 1	LAING	RUN AWAY TRIP	5
JAN. 8, 1943	PURSGLOVE COAL MINING CO.	PURSGLOVE NO. 15	PURSGLOVE	MINE FIRE	13
NOV. 8, 1943	AMERICAN ROLLING MILL CO.	NELLIS NO. 3	NELLIS	EXPLOSION	11
MAR. 25, 1944	KATHRINE COAL MINING CO.	KATHRINE NO. 4	LUMBERPORT	EXPLOSION	16
JAN. 15, 1946	NEW RIVER AND POCAHONTAS CONS. COAL CO.	HAVACO NO. 9	HAVACO	EXPLOSION	15
AUG. 6, 1948	NEW RIVER AND POCAHONTAS CONS. COAL CO.	BERWIND NO. 11	CAPELS	ROOF FALL	6
JAN. 18, 1951	BURNING SPRINGS COLLIERIES CO.	BURNING SPRINGS	KERMIT	GAS EXPLOSION	11
OCT. 15, 1951	TROTTER COAL CO.	BUNKER	CASSVILLE	GAS EXPLOSION	10
OCT. 31, 1951	TRUAX-TRAER COAL CO.	UNITED NO. 1	WEVACO	DUST EXPLOSION	12
NOV. 13, 1954	JAMISON COAL AND COKE CO.	NO. 9	FARMINGTON	EXPLOSION	16
FEB. 4, 1957	POCAHONTAS FUEL CO.	NO. 35	BISHOP	GAS EXPLOSION	37
DEC. 9, 1957	RALEIGH-WYOMING COAL CO.	GLEN ROGERS NO.2	GLEN ROGERS	MOUNTAIN BUMP	5
DEC. 27, 1957	POCAHONTAS FUEL CO.	NO. 31	AMONATE	EAS EXPLOSION	11
FEB. 12, 1958	AMHERST COAL CO.	LUNDALE	LUNDALE	ROOF FALL	6
OCT. 27, 1958	POCAHONTAS FUEL CO	NO. 35	BISHOP	GAS EXPLOSION	22
OCT. 28, 1958	OGLEBAY NORTON COAL CO.	BURTON	CRAIGSVILLE	GAS EXPLOSION	14

Date	Company	Mine	Location	Cause	Deaths
MAR. 8, 1960	ISLAND CREEK COAL CO.	NO. 22	HOLDEN	MINE FIRE	18
NOV. 9, 1962	ISLAND CREEK COAL CO.	NO. 28	VERDUNVILLE	HAULAGE	3
APR. 25, 1963	CLINCHFIELD COAL CO.	COMPASS NO. 2	DOLA	GAS EXPLOSION	22
SEPT. 28, 1964	ISLAND CREEK COAL CO.	NO. 6	BARTLEY	GAS EXPLOSION	3
APR. 30, 1965	MOUNTAINEER COAL CO. (Division of Consolidation Coals Co.)	CONSOL. NO. 9	FARMINGTON	GAS EXPLOSION	4
MAY, 3, 1965	DOROTHY COAL CO.	NO. 1	GARRISON	ROOF FALL	3
OCT. 16, 1965	CLINCHFIELD COAL CO.	MARS NO. 2	SARDIS	MINE FIRE	7
JUL. 23, 1966	THE NEW RIVER CO.	SILTIX	MOUNT HOPE	GAS EXPLOSION	7
SEP. 10, 1966	THE VALLEY CAMP COAL	NO. 3	TRIDELPHIA	HAULAGE	4
MAY 06, 1968	GAULEY COAL & COKE CO.	NO. 8	HOMINY FALLS	MINE INUNDATION	4
AUG. 14, 1968	AMHERST COAL CO.	LUNDALE NO. 1	LOGAN	ROOF FALL	3
NOV. 20, 1968	MOUNTAINEER COAL CO. (Division of Consolidation Coals Co.)	NO. 9	FARMINGTON	EXPLOSION	78
DEC. 12, 1968	BUFFALO MINING CO.	NO. 8B	LYBURN	MINE FIRE	3
JUN. 11, 1971	EASTERN ASSOCIATED COAL CORP.	FEDERAL NO. 2	FAIRVIEW	ROOF FALL	3
JUL. 22, 1972	CONSOLIDATION COAL CO.	BLACKSVILLE	BLACKSVILE	MINE FIRE	9
DEC. 16, 1972	ITMANN COAL CO.	ITMANN NO. 3	ITMANN	GAS EXPLOSION	5
OCT. 02, 1974	COWIN & CO. (CONTRACTORS)	MAPLE MEADOW MINE	FAIRDALE	FALLING MATERIAL	3
OCT. 07, 1974	MONTY BROS. CONST. CO. (CONTRACTOR)	BOLT SEWELL	BOLT	FALL IN SHAFT	3
JUN. 05, 1975	EASTERN ASSOC. COAL CORP.	HARRIS NO. 2	BALD KNOB	RIB FALL	3
NOV. 26, 1975	BETHLEHEM MINES CORP.	NO. 105	CENTURY	ROOF FALL	3
NOV. 07, 1980	WESTMORELAND COAL CO.	FERRELL	UNEEDA	GAS EXPLOSION	5
DEC. 03, 1981	ELK RIVER SEWELL COAL CO.	STILL HOUSE NO. 1	BERGOO	ROOF FALL	3
FEB. 06, 1986	CONSOLIDATION COAL CO.	LOVERIDGE NO. 22	FAIRVIEW	COAL STOR. ENTRAP.	5
MAR. 19, 1992	CONSOLIDATION COAL CO.	BLACKSVILLE NO. 1	WANA	EXPLOSION IN SHAFT	4
JAN. 22, 2003	CENTRAL CAMBRIA DRILLING CO. (CONTRACTOR)	MCELROY MINE	GRAYSVILLE	EXPLOSION IN SHAFT	3
JAN. 2, 2006	ANKER WV MINING CO., INC.	SAGO MINE	TALLMANSVILLE	EXPLOSION AND ENTRAP.	12
APR. 5, 2010	PERFORMANCE COAL CO.	UBBMC MONTCOAL EAGLE	NAOMA	EXPLOSION	29

CPSIA information can be obtained
at www.ICGtesting.com
Printed in the USA
LVOW11s0457270318

571186LV00003BA/582/P